PENNY STOCK INVESTING

Step-by-Step Guide to Generate Profits from Trading Penny Stocks in as Little as 30 Days with Minimal Risk and Without Drowning in Technical Jargon

by Investors Press

Table of Contents

Introduction

"Risk comes from not knowing what you're doing."

Warren Buffett

The world of trading is vast and daunting. It might even be too expensive. Or that is generally how it is perceived. But what if someone were to tell you that you could invest in a company share for less than two dollars? What if someone told you that you could buy shares for even one dollar? Most people would think you were crazy, but this is where a secret and amazing market comes to light. Penny stock investing is the perfect market for people who may have tighter budgets but who also want to get into the world of trading.

However, if you don't know much about penny stock trading, the big question for you may be, *where do I start?* Well, this book will be your guide! Follow this journey of explanations, facts, tips, and tricks that will act as your guide in the jungle of trading penny stock. You might think that this is the same as all the rest of stock trading, but that is absolutely wrong. Instead, there will be a different approach that you'll have to take, and we'll get into the details and show you how.

From strategies you can consider implementing to instructions on how to research effectively, this guide will help you enter into a much cheaper but still rewarding trading platform. There is great potential in penny stock trading, which is why many other companies invest in them. So why not dip your own toes into the marketing sector, and work on potentially growing your income in ways you have never even thought possible?

Later on, you will also learn about the different forms of chart strategies, as well as how to stay safe from scammers and even more. It might even have a few blunt truths that may surprise you, but all in all, it will be an incredibly rewarding journey. At the end of this book, you will have a vital foundational knowledge that can kick-start your journey into investing in penny stocks and learning how to start growing your income even today. As you get more answers and learn more from the lessons, what might have seemed crazy to you at first can now come true, as there are so many businesses available for you to flourish from. All you need is some determination, basic business knowledge, and a great willingness to learn both from here and from those around you. This is not the only source for penny stock investing, but it is a sure-fire way to get you a jumpstart into this journey. You don't have to be scared either, as everyone must start from somewhere. Being a beginner is not altogether a bad thing. It can mean that you will be more willing to take the necessary steps to gather information and research, rather than just dashing into trading blindly and coming out far worse than you started.

In fact, just the fact that you are reading this is making you far wiser than the average investor, who might just like to try their luck on the trading field. And on average, most of them are not so lucky.

If you want to start trading, even as a beginner, find out all you need right here, without having to spend an excessive amount of money on extensive courses or resources. Although penny stock investing has a lot of information surrounding it, it is not as complicated as people try to make it out to be. In fact, the entire world of trading can be complex at times, but really, you just have to learn the essential information, and the more that you know, the better off you will be for it.

Who Is Investors Press?

Investors Press is a group of professionals who are inspired to help individuals that are looking to start their trading journey. With an extensive amount of research and knowledge on trading stocks, we want to share everything that you will need to get started. We have been formulating a thorough and detailed guide to lead beginners and people who are just looking for a refresher on the basics and on the different aspects of investing in penny stocks. We want to help you achieve your financial goals by teaching you step-by-step lessons on how to build an additional stream of income. Your success matters deeply to us, and we hope this guide can lead you on your way to a greater path of trading. We are here to remove the often hampering reliance you may have on stockbrokers, or other unreliable resources, who have shaded the truth with their own marketing tactics, leading up to inevitable failure. This is exactly what we would like you to avoid. And although mistakes are bound to be made, this book will give you an unbiased viewpoint towards penny stock investing, which is exactly what you will need as a beginner.

Chapter 1:
What Exactly Are Penny Stocks?

In the world of investments, everyone tends to think big, such as expensive shares, thirty-story buildings, and multi-million-dollar companies. But, unfortunately, there are many misconceptions that arise when it comes to investing too. Whether it is the reality that only the rich can invest or all shares are costly. However, investing is most certainly not how the movies tend to portray them (i.e., people standing with a glass of wine talking about shares and being rich).

What if we were to tell you that this is not always the case? That, within the surface of investments, lies a deeper truth about how people could earn money? This is where penny stocks come in. They are a different approach from traditional stock investments and may be just what you need in the investment world.

Definition of Penny Stocks

What exactly are penny stocks? Obviously, they are not stocks sold in mere pennies but are a reference to their low price. According to the US Securities and Exchange Commission (SEC), they are normally called "microcap stock" or penny stock. These are normally associated with companies that have a capitalization of less than $250 million or even $300 million. Some businesses certainly have significantly less capital, as they were always intended to be smaller. However, there are even some companies that go below $50 million, and they are typically referred to as "nano cap stocks."

Naturally, the businesses that have smaller capital will be selling shares at a lower price. Penny stocks are normally sold for under five dollars a share. Although it is possible to use exchanges such as the New York Stock Exchange (NYSE) for penny stock trading, the most popular exchanges for penny stocks will be over-the-counter (OTC) transactions. You get these through the electronic OTC Bulletin Board (OTCBB) or even OTC Market Groups that are privately owned (writer et al., 2021).

Penny stocks used to be traded for less than a dollar. However, considering inflation, the SEC tailored it to mean shares that are below five dollars. This matters because it is up to the SEC to protect investors and create equality and fairness on the investor's platform. But it does mean those bad investment choices will still be listed on the SEC, and every so often, scammers do still slip through the cracks. This is a sad but realistic truth, as much as a person would love to have a singular reliable source to trust. But in this modern-day economy, the life of an investor is full of potential; they just have a lot more they will need to learn.

OTC Markets

If you want to have better access to penny stocks, you would probably want to subscribe to the OTCBB. This happens to be a digital or electronic quotation service that was launched and is run by the Financial Industry Regulatory Authority (FINRA). They give you access to the data and quotes of the OTC markets. But be careful about all the offers and specials they may shoot your way; it is best to stay vigilant, especially when you are using this platform.

The reason why you normally cannot find penny stocks on the big exchanges is because they tend to be more volatile and unlikely to meet the requirements to be listed on the big exchanges. Therefore, if you are interested, it would be best to turn your attention to the platforms where you can find penny stocks. However, be careful as a beginner, as penny stocks are not on the normal exchanges, they tend to have increased chances of failing.

How Do Penny Stocks Differ from Regular Stocks?

Although penny stocks do count as regular stocks to a certain degree, a person cannot deny the differences between the smaller shares and the larger shares, as they are even trading on different platforms. The biggest difference between penny stocks and stocks with higher prices is that it takes a lot more effort and work to discover information on the penny stocks. This gets a little harder, especially because you will need to ensure that the information is reliable, as well as up to date. It is hardly worth investing in something over news that has been shared five years ago. In fact, even two years is pushing it. This is because penny stocks do not garner much attention, and they are not required to register with the SEC. This means penny stocks are less likely to be as regulated when it comes to information. A lot of professional stock analysts happen to write about larger public companies, as it is quite easy to find the information necessary. But the same can certainly not be said about penny stocks, so even finding proper professional opinions on a specific form of penny stock may be a more significant struggle.

This means that if you want to become a savvy penny stock investor, you will need to put in extra work, time, and effort in order to get a hold of good and reliable information. This is needed so that you can make the best and most strategic investment decisions. On the other hand, some larger investments, although risky, are easier to navigate when it comes to finding out the necessary information.

When it comes to penny stocks, they normally come at a higher risk than those that are higher priced. Companies that do want to have their stocks listed on specific exchanges are supposed to meet certain standards, such as a total minimum amount of assets or a minimum number of shareholders. Therefore, they can be considered as a certain number of securities that are truly required for the exchange.

This way, investors can hold more confidence in the company just because it managed to make it to the exchange. However, most penny stocks do not qualify. This is because they lack a track record and do not have to meet the minimum listing standards that are normally dictated by the exchanges. It means less information as well as pressure on the company's side and less security for the investor. You will absolutely have to take all this into consideration when planning to invest in penny stocks, as the risk needs to be well worth the reward when you consider investing.

Smaller companies also tend to lack liquidity or at least struggle with it. This means that finding the price within the market and value is far more difficult than with a larger business. Smaller companies are also at a higher risk of being wiped out by a bigger company with their competition, especially if they do not manage to stay up-to-date. Most microcap companies are new, which means they have almost no track records to yet prove themselves to the world and to investors. Some of these businesses might not even have assets, proper revenues, or worse yet, an operation. The low volume of trades latched on top of penny stock trading may make it more difficult for you to sell your shares when the time comes. Because of the low volume trade, it can have a huge impact on the price of the stock. And keep in mind that microcap stocks are a little more susceptible to manipulation or fraud than the larger forms of stocks, merely because they are cheaper to buy and easier to hide the truth.

However, there are still ways and methods of potentially profiting from penny stocks, regardless of whether they are losing value or gaining them. It just means you will have to adapt and change your strategy accordingly to what you believe the stock direction will head toward. This will be explained in depth later in the book.

Penny Stock Tiers

What are tiers in stocks? This is something normally called a "tier market," when investors play favoritism over certain securities that are held within a marketplace. This will result in a higher price for this specific stock group in comparison to others and can sometimes have quite a significant difference.

There are many reasons why this can occur. For example, a group may see a higher potential for higher returns for a specific group, or they may just be exploiting better marketing tactics.

In this modern day and age, any price that fall between one dollar and ten dollars is still seen as quite risky and perhaps even speculative forms of investment. These stocks can drop 50% in value overnight just because of the news or even gain a 100% upward trend if things happen to go well. Therefore, anyone who considers investing in these stocks (normally taking part in day trading) needs to understand that there is always the possibility of incurring a total loss.

However, suppose you do want to put your money into this form of stock. In that case, you will want to have a higher level of security so that you won't necessarily lose the money overnight, and this is where you look at different penny stock tiers.

Tier 1 penny stocks are the ones that you'll want to focus on if you can. This is because they qualify to be listed on exchanges such as NYSE or even NASDAQ. These will be explained in the following chapters. They normally have prices that extend below five dollars a share, but they might even be priced a little higher, considering they are probably more advanced penny stock markets than when they first originally started. Any stocks that fall into this category are still speculative but certainly a whole lot less open to manipulation and fraud, as they do fulfill the higher-level requirements that exchanges ask for. To put it simply, they have a higher capital, a certain number of shareholders, and better financial information has also been provided.

Tier 2 penny stocks are the traditional forms of penny stocks and can literally be priced between one cent and ninety-nine cents. They do not go below one cent, but certain stocks can even be traded at a fraction of a penny, thanks to the digital financial world now available. It is not even uncommon to see stocks that are priced just below a dollar listed on NASDAQ or the NYSE.

However, these companies normally receive a letter, which they usually publicize to the public, that they do need to meet listing requirements (i.e., have their stocks value above one dollar) over a certain amount of time. If they manage it, their stocks will remain listed on the exchange, but if they don't, they will be removed from the list and must move over to the OTC market exchange.

It is critical for stocks to trade above one dollar, as this means that the value never changes to below one cent. However, any stocks that trade below one dollar can even trade down to fractions of a penny.

Tier 3 penny stocks are normally called sub-penny stocks because they are normally below one cent a share. This is where they are merely fractions of a penny and quite low in value. They cannot qualify for NYSE or NASDAQ, which is a massive reason why you should not consider trading with them. They are far from noteworthy and have a low potential, basically an excessively high risk. Losses are more likely to occur with penny stocks that fall under this tier, and you will have to consider your motives if you are interested in investing in stocks that have such low value. Basically, they are not even strong enough to be priced at one cent. This should be proof of the disaster that is likely to await in this company.

Tier 4 penny stocks are when the value of penny stocks is well below a penny (basically $0.0001-0.0009). They are known as trip zero stocks, where they are priced below three zeros.

These stocks can be easily used as vehicles for manipulation. It won't take much to move the market in a different direction. Any purchase can move the stock up by 100%, and this benefits the people who originally purchased the stock. Remember that people will promote this tier, but they are the ones that have stocks in bulk. Meaning any purchases you make, these people will largely benefit from them.

In the end, you will want to focus on penny stocks in tier 1, especially as a beginner, as you are still learning about the markets. When you are more comfortable, it is up to you to invest in tiers below 1, but remember they are a higher risk, and even with experience, it is easy to fall into some of the common traps. It is not always possible to figure out whether a penny stock is legit before it is too late.

However, on average, most professionals try to work with companies that fall under tier one. Therefore, don't hop onto the belief that you are missing out on the impulses of others. Rather, you can consider yourself to be missing out on the common losses and mistakes of others.

Chapter 2:
Are Penny Stocks Worth the
Investment?

If an investment is high risk and extra work needs to be done in order to make good investment choices, you may consider whether penny stocks are worth the investments. Extra risk can make things quite daunting, especially if you are just a beginner.

Indeed, the best way to assess that is to look at the advantages. Understand both the risks and benefits, then you can decide whether the risk is worth the reward.

Looking at both the pros and cons can help make you more unbiased when you make trade decisions and can allow you to deal or be better prepared for disappointments or losses if the risks, unfortunately, fall through. The risks are not an absolute guarantee, but every trader can tell you that they have suffered their fair share of losses when it comes to trading. This is all part of the reality when you take on trading. It will never be smooth sailing. The markets are far too random for that to ever be the reality.

Advantages of Penny Stocks

First, you do not need a big account to start. Considering the low prices of a share, it is a good place to begin when you are possibly low on funds. This means you can break the stereotypes and start early on your investment journey, and one of the wisest choices you can make is to start investing as soon as possible. Time is your biggest ally when it comes to investments.

Diligent work and research will get rewarded. If you learn how to conquer the matters of research and discovery of information on penny stocks, then the rest of your investment journey will be infinitely easier. Researching and doing your due diligence is a key tactic to investing, and it is also the difference between an ignorant investor and a savvy one. In all the books, websites, and even podcasts on investments, there is not likely to be a time where people tell you not to do your own research. Trusting others' information or say so, especially on social media, is a terrible choice, but seeing your efforts rewarded can certainly be listed as an advantage as well.

You can see a potential profit on its way up or down a lot faster than common stocks. With penny stocks, you can profit from them whenever they go up or down. Using a short selling strategy, you can still earn an income despite the possibility that a penny stock value may fail. Short selling is the exact opposite of a normal and traditional stock investment.

There is also the advantage of the potential of gains, as penny stocks are smaller businesses, but they do have the possibility of growing. Seeing small investments grow into larger gains is a great advantage for someone who is starting out in investment. After all, profits is one of the biggest motivating factors for investing. Considering there are higher risks, the promises of higher rewards can motivate one to consider investing. That is if you are more of a risk-taker, considering that there is still the lingering chance that things may go wrong. This advantage is pegged with a critical piece of advice: *Don't invest in what you cannot lose*. This piece of advice will act as a cushion if something does go terribly wrong.

Although it might be difficult to track the research, it is certainly not impossible to track the speed as prices rise or fall. In fact, one will be able to see the changes in price within a matter of days. This is also better for someone who is hands-on with investments. Day-trading is a common strategy when it comes to penny stock investments, so this reality makes day trading a whole lot easier and practical. The only factor is that you will need to learn how to track the patterns occurring in the rising and falling of prices.

Because of the smaller prices, it is easier to buy a variety of stocks. When you add diversity to your portfolio, you spread the risks and significantly boost your chances of success. This can also be accomplished specifically for shorter-term investments. Oftentimes, with larger traders that are changed at a rapid pace, the odds of being able to afford a wide variety is slim. This is easily done when it comes to penny stocks. It can also have a generally positive effect on your portfolio. Most of the time, financial experts consider a person's long-term investments, but they are also aware of the importance of a widely diversified portfolio. Having penny stocks also boosts the chances of increasing your liquidity and mixing up the variety of stocks you have. This certainly strengthens your portfolio. Any factors that can boost your portfolio can wrap up quite an advantage, and it is possible to profit entirely from penny stock investing. Although diversification is recommended, there is a great capability to have diversity in a penny stock and to profit from it. Granted, you play the cards right, and you deal with losses swiftly as well as build up some good wins over time.

Exposure is also quite a good benefit, specifically, exposure to other companies, considering that many large companies happen to buy penny stocks. This is already a good indication because not only can you make connections, but the fact that companies invest in penny stocks is a sign of the potential that lies within. Anyone who has worked in the business world knows that exposure is always good. Having an awareness of other businesses and building connections, especially if you are a part of the business world yourself for your regular day job, can help you create an overall awareness of the financial markets. This is a massive benefit over the fact that you can be a step ahead as a norm with enough practice and work. What you learn from penny stocks, you can also benefit from it in normal investments. Although it is different, penny stock trading teaches you about having grit and having the ability to do thorough research with little resources. You might find normal stocks even easier after taking on penny stocks. That is also quite an advantage.

Disadvantages of Penny Stock

In order to make fair, unbiased, and wise choices, a person will need to look into the drawbacks. This is especially important to help prepare you and combat any of the disadvantages should they occur. Having the ability to boost the advantages and minimize the dangers with counter-tactics is a surefire way to help build your success.

Being aware of the risk can also help you to avoid it. After all, while traversing in a jungle to find the treasure, the more knowledge you have of the danger, the better off you are. Learning to avoid as much of the risk as you can is vital to successful penny stock trading, and learning to take the blow when losses do occur is even better; it is pretty much learning how to take a punch in the financial world. Unfortunately, not many people have what it takes to handle a financial punch.

Most of the companies that have penny stocks happen to be of lower quality. This means that the reputation and sales might not grow much further or could easily fail under too much pressure. Therefore, research must be done about the quality of the company, as well as its plans. If it doesn't manage to adapt or take the brunt of competition, then that is a major red flag. In addition, companies that are also swimming in debt is also definitely considered as a major red flag.

As much as people do not want to hear this, most investors will end up losing some money. This is because they are dabbling in risky markets where regulations are practically non-existent. This allows companies to play by different rules, and oftentimes, can lead to more negative outcomes. It is impossible to leave penny stock trading without some form of loss. You must be prepared for this and be easy on yourself when a loss does take place.

Although it is not completely without regulations, it does mean it plays by different rules. If you want to invest in penny stocks, you will have to learn all the different stockbroker regulations for penny stocks. This is important to keep in mind, as you will not be able to practice the same forms of investments, strategies, or rules in penny stocks as you would do for the average stock. Playing by a different rule book means having a better ability to adapt and think outside of the box. If you want things to be simpler, then consider going for the long-term bigger investments.

There is also a lower trading volume, and penny stocks are traded thinly. This does mean that the number of trades that occur is more or less than the average stocks, which means you must play your cards well. Alongside this comes high volatility, which increases the risk of losing out if you are not careful, but that does not mean volatility in penny stock traders is altogether bad. It may mean there is a higher risk, but later, you will learn the positive aspects of the volatility that you can use to profit from.

Next, this is a risk amongst all stocks and shares in the financial world, but because of penny stock's nature, they can certainly be more prevalent for scams. With the lack of information as well as decreased regulations, it is easier to set up a scam, and you must always be on the lookout for this. Common schemes found on the market are pump and dump (where stock promoters rapidly add support for the stock, including by adding huge investments on their own and marketing the raised price on social media. Then once the price reaches an inflated level, they sell their stocks, and investors have literally lost about all their money.

Another common problem that comes with trading penny stocks is the commission fees tagged alongside it. Be aware that most brokerages have a fair commission rate, but penny stocks are an unfortunate exception. Penny stocks have a much higher commission charge, and you should most certainly check out the fees before signing up for anything. It would be a shame for whatever profits you happen to make to be taken by fees, or worse yet, for you to run at a loss. Commission fees are unfortunately a part of working with a middleman and can hinder your progress when working with cheap shares. Again, be sure that you are using the correct exchange and be updated on the commission fees. Do not move and share trades that can rack up too many commission fees; rather, consider your choices more carefully, and keep track of the fees. They will build up over time and can work as a huge disadvantage if you are not vigilant.

However, this isn't the only picture you should see of penny trading. There is a lot more to the game than what you can see through a rifle scope, but this gives you a great idea to make a balanced, unbiased decision. There is always more than one side to a story, and the same can certainly be said for penny stocks investments. A lot of these risks can be avoided, or if faced, not be allowed to hit too hard. It can also give a clear revelation on whether you are cut out for penny stock trading because day trading and penny stock trading are most certainly not for everyone. Make sure you are motivated and make sure you are up for the task because it is a big one.

There are many stories of the success of people dabbling in penny stocks. Although the risks are quite large, so are the options of reward. Looking up their stories, however, you will see they are filled with hard work, mistakes, dedication, and great knowledge of the market they are working in. Unfortunately, good money does not come easily, and that is just one sad reality that makes most people give up within the investment world.

All this may lead you to ask the question: *Can I honestly make a good amount of money from selling and buying penny stocks?* Unfortunately, it can never be completely guaranteed for you, as no one has the full ability to predict the market (otherwise, you would see people being far more successful).

Trading is not that difficult, but many people do not learn the proper skills they need in order to succeed. Many of the disadvantages listed can, in fact, be avoided through the proper research and time spent to combat them. So, to answer your question, if you do not know or learn how penny stocks work, then you cannot build a foundation strong enough to make yourself successful.

Basically, you can earn money. You have the potential to. But hard work, discipline, and tactics can certainly boost your chances. Of course, trial and error are bound to occur, but that is certainly a guarantee in the world of trading. Everyone makes mistakes here, and those who learn from them are so much wiser.

Penny stock trading is certainly not for anyone who wants it easy; it's for people who want to learn. It is quite a process and has a lot to take into consideration. If you want to stand out from the rest, you need to put in the extra effort. What is worse is that it truly is not so hard to stand out from the majority, purely because the majority do not want to take that time and effort. So, basically, this is a recommendation for you to take the time and effort to stand apart from the rest.

Chapter 3:
The Psychology of a Successful Penny Stock Trader

The biggest battle that occurs is not in the investment field but rather the mindset of a trader. Therefore, it is best to have a look at the mentality behind a successful stock trader as well as the top quality and skills in which a reader should develop to improve their chances of creating a profit. The battle of the mind is a great one, and so it is truly best to be prepared. The mind and emotions are all that make people human. They certainly play a role in every decision you make. But in a gaming platform of trading that works on pure and cold logic, it is best to remove certain elements of emotion if you can for your own benefit.

Trading Psychology Explained

As much as people would love to admit that they do not get emotionally involved when it comes to investing, we all know this is a lie. Specific emotions do have an impact on the decisions, which may defy logic and cause a lot of money to be lost. People have gone to war for money, fought for it, and died for it, so making claims that money has no mental effect on you is not only a lie but is completely impractical.

Alongside normal strategies, it is best to tackle the trading psychology that can vastly improve your success. The two most common emotions that come to play in the world of trading are both greed and fear, but there are many other complex emotions that can sway your thinking. However, to start off with the foundational art of trading psychology, it is time to look at the two most guilty emotions that have the largest impact on your overall decisions.

Greed is considered as the excessive desire to gain wealth and can certainly cloud a person's rational thinking from time to time. It can mean taking unnecessary risks or falling into scams because their marketing was a good way to take away the logic to discern fact from false. Sometimes it is good to take a risk, but it can also be dangerous.

Greed can also cause investors to stay longer in the game than they should in order to squeeze out the most profits. You can see this element taking place in bull markets, where investors throw caution to the wind and speculation runs around like a mad hatter. So greed is not altogether a bad thing, as it can certainly make you work for profit, but it can easily go too far, and this is where you will have to learn the balance.

Fear is the complete opposite, as the thought of risks or possibilities can cause an investor to pull out of the game too quickly. The fear of large losses can cause investors to act far too irrationally, causing panic selling and a major loss of profits as well. Fear is normally never a good emotion to feel when it comes to trading but happens to be amongst the most common emotions felt. Fear often leads to other emotions such as anger, anxiety, and even depression, which are all emotions that are detrimental to your overall health and trading choices.

Therefore, both emotions are certainly not ideal for anyone. However, one emotion that tags alongside both is regret. This issue can add to impulsive decisions after mistakes have already been made, which adds salt to the wound.

Importance of Knowing Trading Psychology

Training yourself in trading psychology can help you reduce any forms of error in judgment that could be made, specifically those that are driven by emotions and reactions. This is recommended, especially as a beginner, where everything can certainly feel a lot like a rollercoaster. Preparing yourself beforehand is critical to help you not get overwhelmed. Is it possible to think like an artificially intelligent robot? No, you should expect many of these emotions to arise, but how you handle them is all part of whether you win or lose in the trading world. In fact, one of the biggest losses is most likely caused by choices based on someone's emotions. To avoid unnecessary risk, take extra time and patience to master your emotions.

Mastering your emotions means having the ability to detect patterns and strategies without being biased towards any particular investment and understanding when to hold, despite fears, and when to sell. It is a matter of managing your emotions. This avoids a common no-hold and hope mentality you may find amongst many investors.

No-hold and hope are when you are overstaying your welcome in a bad trade that is occurring. It is holding onto the hope of better trades even if it is unlikely to happen. This is quite a common mistake that is so easily avoidable if only you did not get emotionally involved. This normally involves an investor creating a strategic plan but then failing to keep to it in hope that holding onto the investment will pan out in the end despite signs showing drastically the opposite. Learning how to manage your emotions in order to avoid this is critical for your overall success.

Your ability to manage risk will also vastly improve. As you remove emotional factors, you can replace them with logic and facts, as this is the game you must play in the investor's world. You may make choices to stay or pull out when it is far more practical than if you were to run on greed or fear. It makes a lot of sense when it is mentioned, but when it comes to real-life application, it is infinitely harder.

Personality Types in Trading

First, you need to identify what your personality type is when it comes to trading. Each person approaches investments with a different attitude, and identifying yours will help you overcome any weakness that comes alongside this former personality. There are two primary examples:

Firstly, there is a rigid trader. This is a person who tends to follow patterns they detect as well as rules. They also tend to follow plans to a T. Although this can be helpful for anyone who has a good plan, if the plan were to backfire, it could easily work against this personality type. They can easily struggle with emotions such as greed and fear; greed in sticking to the plan even if it is not feasible under the belief everything will work out or fear that adapting can somehow ruin the entirety of the plan.

Secondly, there is the flexible trader. This trader is far more adaptive to changes, making edits to their plan in the middle of a trade. Although this can also be an admirable quality for a volatile trade, this trader is at risk of changing plans too quickly or veering off course into a great loss. However, the emotion of fear does tend to be more prominent with this personality trait. A willingness to adapt plans under the slightest change can cause issues.

Tips to Improving Trading Psychology

What exactly can you do to improve your mental approach to trading? Well, you must get yourself into the correct mindset, specifically, the right trading mindset. You must remind yourself constantly that stock prices are not personal. They work purely on statistics, numbers, and logic alone. There are no feelings of consideration for the investors, just numbers, and this is what you must remind yourself. This is a battle of strategy and logic, not fear or greed.

Do not give trades a personality or life, which may sound strange, but it is entirely possible when you invest a lot of time and effort into doing research. A trade, especially in penny stocks, will always be short-and-sweet and should be approached as such.

Patience is key. Any wise investor will tell you this. Having the ability to wait, or stop yourself before making an impulsive decision, is a great idea. Not only can this stop you from falling into some of the most common scams in investments, but it can boost your success at a rapid rate. Patience allows you to take a deep breath and step away from emotions that may be overpowering you at this point and time. It is giving your mind a break before making any decisions, and it is giving yourself proper time to think things through. Oftentimes, the most common trick scammers use is a sense of urgency and impatience, so already having the patience is slipping the hooks of one of the common investor scams.

Education not only improves your strategies but also affects trading psychology. The more knowledge you have on both the mental battles and the physical battles of investing, the better off you are. How else would you identify investors falling into "fear of missing out" unless you know about it? It is like anger: the best way to gain control of your anger is to realize you are angry. The same can be said for education and investments. The more you know, the better you are at dealing with it on an emotional level. People also stress about what they do not know, or they are afraid. Getting to know as much as you can about trading is certainly one of the greatest solutions you can use to tackle the emotional reactions to trading.

Next is to prepare your mind for the best and worst scenarios. As the one saying goes, "Hope for the best and prepare for the worst." This way, you can have the joy of succeeding and the cushion in case you lose. Imagine yourself winning in the trade, and this can certainly motivate you to work harder. But leave space to imagine yourself losing, allowing yourself to prepare for the worst and disarming that nasty element of surprise if things don't pan out for you. It is terrible to have to recommend this, but the shock factor will not have such a significant effect on you if you practice this technique. It may seem simple, but few people mentally approach a trade this way, as many people prefer not to focus on all the possible negative aspects.

Furthermore, you may find yourself disillusioned when looking at the numbers on the screen. You must keep reminding yourself that you are working with real money here. This allows you to practice more caution in your decisions and more caution if you tend to be more of a risky person. Obviously, if you struggle with fear, you do need to focus on the fact that money is just that: money. Remove the emotional connections you may have with it.

Study Habits of Successful Traders

Apart from trading psychology, there are studying habits, which are tricks people use to improve their knowledge. Keep in mind that everyone has their own methods of studying, so choose your specific style and go with it. Whether it is finding a quiet place in your house, or being among people in a cafeteria, do whatever floats your boat. There is also the common study term known as VARK: visual, auditory, reading, and kinesthetic, where you learn by seeing, hearing, reading, touching, or a combination of them all. It is best to discover the optimal ways you learn to save you a lot of time and effort.

Then the next step is to practice, whether that is working out strategies and trying them out on simulators or studying the terminology. Practice makes perfect and is certainly very necessary when starting out with investments as with any other money-making strategy. As much as one could wish for an easy money-making method, anything worth your time will not be easy. But it doesn't mean it's impossible; you just need some time and effort to practice, discover, and learn. Better yet, find yourself a trader to follow and learn from if you can. Watching their strategies and understanding the decisions they make can certainly help you build your own methods and practices.

Observe the progress you have over time when it comes to your trading. Assess what has improved and look back to the prior strategies you made. Analyze them and be critical. What worked? What did not work? Where can you improve? Where have you already improved? In order to learn from your prior mistakes, it is best to consider keeping a trading journal. It might take more time and effort, but keeping records of your journey can certainly help you identify what you did wrong and what you did right. Focus on asking yourself the 5 W's and 1 H questions: where, what, why, when, which, and how. An example would be: *What went wrong? When did the trade go south? Why did it go south? How can I prevent this in the future? Which trader/news/source caused the trade to suddenly change direction? Where should I focus on improving my trade?*

Staying Focused After Losses

Perhaps the most critical time to practice good trading psychology is when facing losses, as that is bound to happen for anyone who becomes an active trader. Be aware that just because you suffer a loss doesn't mean you are automatically kicked out of the game. It depends on how well you reacted to the loss and how well you spread your losses as well. But a loss is loss, and a person who trades cannot escape the inevitable reality that this will happen sometimes.

However, when facing a loss, it is best not to wallow too deeply. Consider this merely a learning curve and stick with the trading plan you have at hand unless you identify a critical flaw. But it is best to focus on something physical and logical at a time when emotions can be running rampant. Rather than letting loose of any strategy, cling to it just a little tighter.

Keep an eye on market trends, as this can help identify any losses that may occur in the future and help you pull out before it is too late. Remember to place stop orders on your trade where automatic orders are triggered when the stock you have happens to reach a specific price, and place a mental stop in your mind. In other words, pull out and take a break if you need to. This does not mean you have to fully stop, but if a loss is truly heavy, it is sometimes better to take a step back rather than fall into panic and fear and make heavier losses than initially drawing out for a little while in the first place. It is much like taking a step back and an extra-long breath when getting mad at someone—same idea. Allowing yourself to breathe after a long bout of stress and loss is the perfect idea for someone who is just beginning in trading.

But that does not mean your journey ends here. Carry on with the idea that you are still learning. In trading, you will always be learning. Whether it is about the latest trends, technology, or software programs, the world is ever-evolving. And so the world of investing, even in penny stocks, is also changing. Therefore, it is best to stay disciplined in this aspect.

Emotions That Could Ruin Day Trading

If you are participating in day trading, you need to be aware of the most common emotions that could kill your success. It is best to tackle them one by one and be aware of them as you start. Working to build up your resilience and strength against them will certainly help your journey. They are:

- Boredom. Rather than wasting any time, use the free moments you must learn more about day trading. But if you do happen to get distracted due to boredom, you will start taking some unnecessary risks that aren't worth it in the long haul. It is basically taking a gamble, and we all know day trading isn't a casino, so don't take that risk. Learn to avoid boredom by taking certain times off, travel, and even go watch YouTube videos to have a more fun learning experience. There are some incredible teachers out there dedicated to teaching the craft in a way that doesn't inspire you to take a nap. YouTube is a great place for this. Watching motivational videos are also a great way to keep yourself on track and committed to doing the work you need to do.

- Depression. This is a far more serious challenge you may have to face and something that is sadly common amongst traders and investors. Taking losses is not easy for anyone, and some have gone too far when it comes to handling these negative emotions. Many traders can even get depressed after making a large loss or a couple of smaller losses. Therefore, it is wise to approach the financial market with a lot more knowledge and understanding of the risks before even taking a step into trading. Knowledge can help prepare you for both joy and disappointment. Furthermore, only open a trade if you know you are comfortable losing. If you are not willing to even consider the thought of a loss, then it may be time to reconsider whether you are cut out to be a trader. Whether you need some more time and advice, don't allow yourself to be emotionally hindered at a bad trade. Everyone has their bad days, but their success lies in the factor of how they react to them. This is the most common difference between people who fail and people who succeed. It is not how they respond through the good times, but how they respond through the difficult ones.

- Doubt. When numbers and odds flip so quickly, even the most experienced trader may go through bouts of doubt every so now and then. It is a good idea not to second guess every single choice you make. If you walk into trading with an open mind and are willing to learn without dwelling, it can certainly help to reduce a lot of the doubt you may experience. Doubt is a dangerous emotion because it is a close relative to fear. Doubt can cause you to make wrong mistakes just as easily as fear can, so it is best never to regret any decisions you have made, even if they were the wrong ones. The only time you are ever allowed to doubt yourself is when you guessed the total calories of that chocolate bar from a week ago. But steer clear of doubting in a trade; it will only cause more trouble than it is worth.

- Fear. A person could say this is the most popular emotion you will find running rampant in the marketplace. There is even a common concept called "fear of missing out" (FOMO) that refers to you buying an asset against all logic simply because the price is rising or falling, and people are jumping onto the same purchases as well. Fear plays alongside peer pressure, and you tend to see fear at its strongest when it comes to cryptocurrency, a market far more volatile than even penny stocks. Another fear is the one where you are scared to even enter a market. This means you do all your analysis and never find yourself fully satisfied stepping into a trade, no matter what the potential. This means you probably miss out on a lot of major opportunities and profits within the market system.

- Anger. This normally occurs when your doubts and fears come true. This is the time you should take a step back and a deep breath, as there is normally nothing you can do about it now. There is no use stressing about matters that are now beyond your control. The best thing you can do is learn from your mistake, even writing it down in a trading journal, and walk away. This is far wiser than trading in anger, as it can throw all rationality and logic out of the window. This is commonly called "revenge trading," where you try to make up for the losses you have made by taking even riskier trades. And in most of those trades, you are far more likely to make a loss than if you were calm.

- Anxiety. This tends to be a recovery period after a terrible trade. The next few trades you make will probably be filled with anxiety. Remember to relax! It is best to avoid anxiety; otherwise, you can pull out too early in the trade or fail to come up with a good strategy. If you are anxious, then consider starting small with your trades again until you build up sufficient confidence in your skills again. Anxiety again is a close relative of fear, so it normally gets triggered with that emotion. If you struggle with anxiety beyond the trading arena, then it is best to learn how to deal with it in all aspects as far as you can muster. Not only will this improve your overall mental life, but also the skills and decisions you make on a trade.

All of these are quite dangerous emotions. You should consider speaking to a professional if need be in order to help deal with them. Some are easily changed, but others, such as depression or anger, may need some help. You must be honest with yourself, and making wise decisions will certainly help your success in the investing world.

One emotion, greed, though it can be bad for you, can also help grow your penny stock price, but it is certainly bad for succeeding at trading. On the other hand, your motivation to earn profits can help you overlook some daunting risks that many others won't even consider taking on. But this is why it is best to have a healthy balance, both of motivation to earn money but also a healthy amount of fear of risks. That way, you can take risks but pull out of the game if it does happen to get a little too dangerous.

Therefore, it is so important for you to set clear goals. There is no black and white trading to operate investments and trades. If there was, everyone would certainly be successful in trading. Rather, it is like treading uncertain waters. Finding the balance and control of your emotions takes time, practice, and experience.

Mental Tricks That Separate You from Being A Potential Winner to A Definite Loser

There are certainly a lot of mental steps and tricks to learn in trading psychology, so what separates you from those who constantly have pitfalls and mental traps they are not altogether aware of? Here are some things you need to look out for in order to stand out from the average investor.

Firstly, avoid analysis paralysis. When you first start off in the trading world, you will have to soak in a lot of new information. The information tends to come in all forms, shapes, and sizes, including some from your own personal background. Using this information, you will start your practices in the world market. Your first trade can certainly be quite scary despite everything that you know. Hopefully, your first trade goes smoothly, and the money comes rolling in. However, if you are unlucky, then you will start to understand why so many traders tend to give up or fail. This is called facing loss, and your first loss can and will certainly hurt.

The trick here is to get beyond the despair, hurt, or disbelief that tends to crouch at your door as a trader. So how exactly do you do this? Well, consider that you just spent a couple of hours or even weeks crafting an amazing trading strategy. But when you test it out, only one of six trades world. Any savvy trader will know that patience and setting up a large enough sample of the traders will truly reveal how effective the strategy is. But someone who is a beginner may get paralyzed and pull out of the game due to doubt and fear (the common emotions) before even seeing the true potential of the strategy they took to develop. This can quickly lead to getting disheartened, as nothing seems to work, which forces people to quit before they are even properly in the game.

It is best to accept that the market is random. By understanding this factor, you will have a better mentality that can lead to profits. You can spend all the time in the world working on predicting the markets, allowing you to feel a sense of control, but sometimes, even so, predictions fail, and so do analyses. Accepting that this is how the market works can allow you to release a lot of the frustration that builds up when you try and predict the markets. It's just not worth that stress. Predicting is good; despairing over a failed prediction isn't.

Here is some bad news. It only takes one trader to invalidate the analysis you have made, especially when it comes to penny stock investments, where trades can so easily get influenced. Now it doesn't mean you will necessarily fail over an invalidated analysis, but it does mean that you should not place all of your trust on it. It can only take one person to help grow or decrease the value of the stock, depending on how much they evidently invest in or remove. So again, it is best to remove any emotional attachment you have for the market and do not take it personally if it does not head in the direction you thought it would. Otherwise, you may see your profits cut a lot shorter or even at a loss because you followed your analysis with utmost dedication.

Shutting out the noise is another good mentality to take on. What exactly is the noise? This occurs when you have too much information from too many sources about trading, specifically drowning out your own thoughts, strategies, and ideas. Basically, signing up for newspapers, spam emails, and feeds giving off the latest tips and tricks will only confuse you more. The best way to drown out the noise is to do the research on trading when you want to and to occasionally ignore what people may send you. A lot of these newsletters, emails, and updates will contradict each other because they are based on a variety of different people's opinions, so it is certainly best to develop your own and move on. Sure, it is great to learn from others, but to get flooded with the next tip or trend without you actively seeking it out can cause a lot of confusion, which will cloud your path.

It is easy to say you understand there is a risk. Anyone does that when climbing on a rollercoaster or eating a piece of bad chicken without much thought of the consequences. But thinking things through and grasping the understanding of what the risk will cost you is important. You may say that you are willing to take on the risk of the trades (inwardly, as you still do not want to lose the money—who does?), but this will only be reflected when you happen to suffer a loss. This can trigger a lot of dangerous emotions mentioned before, especially if you were not truly ready for the loss, so we cannot stress enough how important it is to accept the randomness of the market. However, again, this is only going to work if you can afford to lose the money. If you cannot, then naturally, you are going to be emotionally invested no matter what. Therefore, do not invest what you cannot afford to lose.

Learning when to take the profits is another mental trick that can help you with penny stock trading. It sounds easy enough, except that many traders get hooked with the possibility of what could happen next. This is a similar mentality of a gamble, where many people continue to place bets after having a few wins just out of the pure thrill and possibility of earning more. A good trader knows when to pull out of the game despite what promising opportunities may lie ahead, as this avoids taking on unnecessary losses again. Figuring out the times to walk away will be doing yourself a massive favor.

Finally, realizing and admitting when you are wrong is another great tactic when it comes to stock trading. This may sound strange, but an unwillingness to admit defeat or mistakes from time to time can do you a massive disservice. On the other hand, when you admit that you are wrong, you are also acknowledging a willingness to learn from it. When you learn to accept these factors, it can save you a lot of time and money, which will allow you to move on.

You need to develop a winning attitude. What exactly does this mean? It means you get into a mental place when you approach the market with a can-do attitude. You should fully accept what the market throws at you, but also what the market is willing to provide, reducing the unrealistic expectations that tend to take place left, right, and center amongst a lot of people. This does mean not allowing doubt or fear to get in the way. There is nothing wrong with acknowledging risk and dealing with it if it does come true, but doubt and fear can easily pull away from the winning attitude you need in order to stand out.

Winning at a trade has very little to do with the system you use, the equipment, and internet speed. It all comes down to the responsibility you take with the results and acceptance of what you receive from the market. It may not always be positive, but having the endurance and grit to push things through will get you further than merely training in facts and knowledge.

This is as much of a mental battle as it is a physical one, and this is something you will have to accept.

Keep training yourself mentally. As much as this is a battle of strategy, it is also a mental battle. Those who are aware of this factor tend to have higher rates of success. This is because they can play on the emotional waves of others while steering clear of their own. Understanding the behavior of common investors will help you identify a lot of the volatility that goes in penny stock marketing, as well as help you diffuse a scam. It also keeps you away from making irrational choices, so we cannot stress enough how important the battle of the mind is with penny stock marketing.

Remember to stay on the positive side. As much as a trader's life can sink into pessimism, allow your eternal optimist to flourish just a little regardless of whether bad things happen. The ability to see the bright side even in a bad trade can get you far.

Chapter 4:
The Basics of Investing in Penny Stocks

The first step to building a house is the foundation, and so the same could be said for learning or building in any category. Learning the basics of penny stock investing is about knowing the foundation, which is one of the most critical components of building towards your success. Next, of course, you want to build up for yourself an empire of trading experience and hopeful profits. But you must start somewhere, right? Sometimes shaving everything down to the basics is what you need exactly to benefit from making the right trading decisions.

How The Stock Market Works

Stock markets do carry a certain element of risk with them, but one thing that has been proven time and again is that if a disciplined approach is taken with a stock market, then it is certainly one of the best methods to build a person's net worth.

Stock markets can be considered a common marketplace where people can buy and sell shares in companies. Stocks themselves happen to represent the ownership of a company, and the prices are set depending on the supply and demand in the market. It also can be called equity or share. Therefore, the value of a share depends on the level of activity that derives from both buyers and sellers. Stocks also act as a form of representation to have a certain amount of claim on its assets (what the business specifically happens to own), as well as some of its earnings.

Companies often want to raise capital larger than a bank loan would allow. Furthermore, they do not want the burden of having to repay a bank with high-interest ratings. This is a common reason why they issue shares in order to increase scalability without creating excessive debt. Raising capital is a great way to boost the growth of the business and profits, but sometimes businesses do need large amounts of money to start. Capital growth is the primary reason why companies issue shares. In order to grow at a faster pace, you do need to raise funding in a fast and efficient way.

There are two main forms of stock: common and preferred. The main difference that does occur between the two normally involves voting rights. Common shareholders hold the right to have a certain say and vote in the meetings, such as when the board of directors or even auditors are voted upon. Preferred shares do not have such voting rights, but they do receive a higher preference than those in common shares and are more likely to receive dividends or assets if the business were to liquidate.

Stock Exchange

The stock exchange works like a second-hand store in real life. This is the platform where existing owners of the shares can sell them to potential buyers. Buyers do not interact directly with the companies on this platform but rather with the shareholders themselves. This emphasizes the reality that public companies normally don't have as much control over who purchases their shares.

Listing Shares

When a company is first launched, it will need a large amount of capital and can get it from operations such as a bank loan, but then again, why get into debt when you can sell your shares to the public? This is normally done through an initial public offering (IPO) and can change the status on which the company officially stands. Normally, the IPO offers early investors the option to cash out and the ability to reap handsome rewards, which is all well said and done if the business is successful.

Once the company's shares are indeed listed on a stock exchange, this is when the shares can fluctuate as both traders and investors alike work on assessing the value.

How Share Prices Are Set

The most common area where the price of a share tends to be set is in the auction process. This is where buyers and sellers place bids and offers to buy or sell the shares. The bid is the price that the buyers place and the amount they are willing to pay, whereas the offer is the amount the person is willing to sell for. The supply and demand determine the average price for which shares are commonly sold for.

There are many different forms of ratios or metrics that can be used in order to value the stock, but the most common formula is the Price-Earnings or even (PE) ratio. This is a great way to figure out more about the analytics side when it comes to the financial world of the company.

Returns on Stock Investments

Returns on stock investments, otherwise known as ROIs, work by figuring out the profit or loss made with a specific investment. A person can normally do this by subtracting the final investment amount from the original cost you had invested. Evidently, if your answer happens to be positive, you have made a profit. But if the answer is in the negative, then you have suffered a loss. You can also calculate the number of dividends you have received, as this will add to your profits.

Stocks are normally classified in two ways. One is known as market capitalization, which is the total market of the company's shares. The other is by sector, where the stocks are classified by the Global Industry Classification Standard. The Global Industry Classification Standard is the industry taxonomy that was created and launched in 1999 by the MSCI as well as Standard & Poor. This was used for the global community of finances.

Where Penny Stocks Trade

Now you may like to know what direct sources to look for. Below are some of the top listed marketplaces. What you do need to understand is that each brings its own unique advantages to the table, but they also have downfalls, as there is no perfect system after all. It is best for you to decide what works for you and what risks you are indeed willing to put up with. Some of the exchanges listed are not even recommended, but rather here to create an awareness of what you should consider avoiding as a beginner and even as an experienced trader.

NASDAQ Small Cap Market

NASDAQ Capital Market, which was known until the year 2005 as NASDAQ Small Cap Market, has a primary list of small-cap stocks, but the name changed to reflect a big shift in focus. Companies listed here have the desire to raise their capital. It means that small businesses did not have such a burden to be listed on this marketplace and could also grow through the NASDAQ listing.

The advantages are that you can invest after-hours extended trading hours, in comparison to the NYSE that can only manage trading with the open hours of the day. After hours with NASDAQ means you can trade up to 8 p.m. in the evening at times.

There is also online automation using this platform, where you can trade from the comfort of your own home. Having the ability to access this platform online removes the need to administer trades on behalf of the investor. Rather, the investor can take a lot of the trading responsibility into their own hands. However, this does allow a certain level of higher liquidity and more control over the choices you want to make.

However, keep in mind that Nasdaq does not carry the same level of prestige, and many of the listings are known to be quite volatile. Furthermore, keep in mind that penny stocks bring disadvantages of their own.

OTC-BB

OTB-BB stands for over-the-counter bulletin board, in which you secure trades via a broker-dealer network. This moves away from the centralized exchange centers and can involve equities, debt instruments, and other forms of derivatives. Taking away the middleman is always an advantage for people who prefer to stay anonymous, and you can find a lot of the equities that are not listed on the current exchanges. These equities are normally called over-the-counter equity securities.

Greater care needs to be practiced when working on the OTC marketplace, as the security and regulations are indeed far looser. This means that scams are quite common, as well as businesses that frequently fail.

Amex

Amex is an iconic and global financial brand that has racked up billions of dollars in revenue and has thousands of employees across the globe. It is popular and quite advanced in years.

Amex is a relatively solid choice considering its long history but never an absolute guarantee. There is still a consistent growth in revenue and taking strides to remain competitive against other growing markets. It is also starting to take on a more digital focus.

However, there has been a slight fall in the results of the year's earnings, and this can be quite concerning for investors, as Amex is a little behind in the competition. In addition, it is facing a lot of challenges as a card provider, and the dividend returns are also quite small in using this platform. These are all things to take into consideration.

Canadian Markets

The Canadian stock markets have been doing remarkably well and are rich in resources, as well as having quite a sound financial sector. As safe as the economy and situation appear, it is best to approach them with an unbiased viewpoint.

Firstly, the Canadian currency is strong, and trades are going well so far in Canada. As mentioned before, Canada's banking system is incredibly sound. There are plenty of resources, especially in companies and stock exchanges. This makes it incredibly tempting to invest in penny stocks in this sector.

But be aware: there is a lack of diversification, which means that there are many sectors in this industry that are sorely lacking. Moreover, it is still a small market, so even if you were to consider investing, it might be best to diversify your portfolio in other markets as well. There is also a currency risk despite it being strong. If inflation levels rapidly start to rise, there will be a lot of heat on the economy as well as on Canadian banks.

Pink Sheets Penny Stocks—Steer Clear!

This is mentioned here only for the reality that it is not recommended at all. Pink sheet stocks have been considered good investments, as they work as a quotation service and not an exchange for trading OTC. However, here comes the big problem: pink sheet stocks are thinly traded and lack a lot of liquidity. Many of the companies using pink sheet penny stocks are quite worthless. To put it plainly, it is just not worth the risk to invest with pink sheets penny stocks, as you are far more likely to suffer a loss than making a gain on this platform.

Penny Stocks Straight from the Companies

Investing directly with the company removes the safety of regulations that are still in place despite being penny stocks. There is absolutely no guarantee of a fair valuation, and you are far more likely to get scammed or ripped off. There are too many companies that are scraping by the edge of their teeth and the investments coming in from ignorant bystanders hoping to get some return. The odds are too small, and you have no proper protection from the investment you made.

Penny Stocks Over the Phone

This is just a bad idea. Firstly, you can never properly verify who you are talking to on the phone, and secondly, it is likely to be a scam. A person should not have to explain why trading penny stocks over the phone should *never* be considered.

Buying Penny Stocks: Basic Elements

There are some basic elements you will need to know and check up on when buying penny stocks. In order to proceed, you will need the following details to complete your order:

Firstly, the ticker system. This is the name of the company, which you will probably need to know. You will then need to know the market on which the penny stocks are trading. Considering you want to target a specific company, it is best to know where to work on the exchanges after all.

You will also need to decide on the number of penny stocks you want to buy. This is typically considered the volume of shares and the amount you have in your budget. For example, if you have $2000, and the company sells shares at $0.50, then you will want to order about 4000 shares if you are buying all of them at $0.50.

You will also want to set a market or limit price. This is for trade orders or shares that you are not completely sure of the price. In order to make sure the trade price will go through, it is best to limit the price. For example, by setting it at $0.70 per share, you will not pay any more for those shares. Therefore, if they are selling it at a ridiculously high price, you avoid getting ripped off from the company.

You can also decide on the duration of your order. Normally, market orders do not require a form of duration, but if you are willing to wait for your share to reach the ideal price, then you can have your order fulfilled when it hits the trading floor.

Limit orders, on the other hand, need a duration, and you will also get an additional limit order duration.

Next, you will want to figure out the total cost. It is best to consider not just the price of the shares but also the commission costs and any other fees that may come alongside it. Again, having a budget and estimation of the prices can help prevent any nasty surprises from coming your way.

Then you will need an open order. This is the duration before your order expires, and it is certainly considered to be open. It is best to keep an eye on your open orders, which should be easy to check if you have an online brokerage account. It is a great way to check and see the shares you have purchased and the price you have paid for them.

Selling penny stocks involves the same elements as buying stocks, just in a matter of slight reversal. Instead of paying for them, you are obviously selling them.

Picking A Stockbroker

Considering they are the middleman, picking your stockbroker is quite important, and there are two types of stockbrokers you need to be aware of. They differ in a few areas and depending on your goals, you will want to choose different stockbrokers.

The first is the discount broker. Naturally, you pay a smaller fee for them, but it normally means they simply follow your orders. You will have to do your own research, and any decision you make will reflect nothing on them.

The second is the full-service broker. You pay a higher fee for them, but they will spend more time giving advice, direction, and drawing up a portfolio plan for you. This is certainly more suited for clients who are invested in larger portfolios and thus are willing to pay higher commission fees.

Broker Criteria

How do you decide on the right broker for you? There are several steps you can take for this. Firstly, you will have to determine your own requirements. It does depend on your situation and circumstances. It is also ideal to have one broker instead of three or more, no matter what the temptation may be to add variety.

You will have to check out commission fees and make sure it is affordable for you and that the speed at which the broker works for order execution is to your liking. You will evidently want a broker that is reliable and understands the policies of penny stocks, as not every broker may know how to deal with them.

You will need to check out the broker's accessibility if issues should arise, as well as the level of customer service. If customer service is difficult, then it will be a massive pain to work with them.

Furthermore, it is best to check out a customer's research and their available tools. How well are they able to stay up to date with the trends, and what tools do they have available? Being up to date is important, but that does not mean all brokers adopt this policy.

Candlestick

Another tool to add to your kit is the candlestick, which is a type of price chart used for technical analysis. It displays both the high, low, open, and closing prices of the security for a specific period. They tend to show investors whether the closing price of a market was lower or higher than what the opening price was, which is critical to understanding how the stock market is truly faring. Thus, it is excellent for traders who are specifically looking for chart patterns that may occur.

The reason why it is called a candlestick is because of its candlestick appearance on the market itself. The name originally came from Japanese rice merchants and other traders who were far ahead in recording financial management before it became popularized in America.

The top of the candlestick represents the highest price of the day, whereas the end of the candlestick represents the lowest price of the day. The thicker centerpiece at the top represents the opening and closing price, and so does the thicker piece at the bottom. The body of the candlestick is either black or red if the stock closes at a lower price, but it is white or green if it closes at a higher price.

The shadow of the candlestick represents the day's high and low moments, especially in comparison to how a stock market opens or closes.

Ultimately, the candlestick represents the impact of the investor on security prices and is more than often used for technical analyses, as it is directly linked to the company in the financial aspect of its stocks. This is a handy tool to use as a penny stock investor, and you should learn all about it before even setting your foot into investing. Candlesticks are used for any technique when it comes to trading many forms of financial assets, such as stocks or even foreign exchanges.

When a candlestick is white or green, it is normally a sign that there is a lot of buying pressure building upon a particular stock. This tends to be an indicator that a certain stock is "bullish." But it is important to look at the candlestick within the context of the overall market, as it can give a good indication as to why you should or should not consider investing in it after all. When you see a lot of red/green candlesticks, that is an indicator that there is overall a lot of selling pressure and an indication that a market is in a "bearish" state. What does it mean when a market is in a "bearish" or "bullish" state?

A bull market is when a stock is starting to rise and trade on a more continuous basis. This is normally an ideal scenario to get caught up in as a trader, especially if you are focusing on the long strategy.

A bearish market indicates a drop in the prices, where a lot of people want to sell the stock. And believe it or not, a person can also benefit from this through short selling. But this form of profiting is far riskier and will require a lot more experience in order to be able to pull off something such as that.

Now coming back to the candlestick: Traders can take advantage of candlestick charts to effectively analyze literally any cycle of trading that occurs at any point and time in the day. You can even use it to analyze a minute of trading or up to an hour. That is all up to you to use at your discretion and wisdom. In short, there is a lot you can learn when it comes to candle charts, and their usefulness will not be diminishing any time soon.

Two-Day Candlestick Pattern

These are more based on short-term strategies from the information given on candlestick patterns. These trading patterns normally signal a reversal in trends, where the first candlestick has a short body and the second towers over the first. This is normally called a "bullish engulfing pattern," and is good to keep an eye out for. The "harami" is the name called for the complete reversal of this trade, where the first candle completely towers over the first.

Three-Day Candlestick Pattern

This is commonly called an "evening star," where it starts with a bearish pattern and quickly turns into an uptrend. The second candle shoots upwards but has a narrower body, which is an indicator for less volume. The third candlestick, though, tends to come at the middle part of the first candlestick. The reversal, called a "morning star," is a more bullish pattern.

It is important to make sure you completely understand what is going on with a candle chart. Take your time studying them before investing, even practicing out these tools or techniques mentioned via paper trading first before putting any real money into it. However, a candlestick chart pattern is advantageous to know and is probably one of the major tools that traders use to help win their success.

Chapter 5:
The Trader's Toolbox

Every person needs a toolkit for their practice. Being a trader is no exception to this rule. To become a penny stock investor, you will need a tool kit to refine your craft and trade penny stocks effectively. In summary, it is boosting your chances for success.

http://finance.yahoo.com

One of the easiest tools to use is websites such as http://finance.yahoo.com. It is one of the simplest, free tools to use to check on the percentage of gainers. Sometimes, however, considering this is a free tool, it may mean that the figures are not always as accurate, as less time and effort is spent on their accuracy.

http://www.stockopedia.com

This is another great free tool for you to use. It gives simplified charts and other forms of information for you to use in your journey as a trader. There is also a paid version available, so if you like the free version enough, then you can consider taking on the paid one, especially if you would like to know about all the financial credentials of a certain amount of stock.

http://freestockcharts.com

This is a platform that is run by the Worden brothers

and is known to be the backbone of TC-200 200 software. It is extremely useful for technical analysis, and you can even get greater detail if you pay for the premium version. Again, this all depends on your budget, but it is great to consider tools that can just make your life easier when it comes to manners of research and analysis of the specific stock. It will make your journey more successful, as you will be able to spot more dangers as well as opportunities.

http://stockcharts/com

Much like the tool above, it is a great charting tool, and again, has greater details in the premium version, as to be expected as the developers would like to make some money from the equipment theory they are creating.

http://www.sec.gov

This is a great platform to keep a watch out for and search for sec filings that you know you are looking for. To top it off, this is a reliable site, so you will likely find what you are looking for here. Nothing is more destructive to a person's success than unreliable information, so it is always best to double-check any tools and sources you are using for your trading.

http://stocktwits.com

This is a website that gets ideas when trading different types of stocks.But be careful who you believe when using this site and don't ever trade with someone else's trading idea unless you fully understand their strategy and have the same conclusion for yourself. It is great to draw ideas from those who have been in the game longer, but ultimately, it is your money that you are risking. Therefore, it is best that you definitely stay responsible for any plans that you undertake.

http://www.microcapsearch.com

This is a cool tool that is useful if you would like quick access to other websites that provide information about stock and important data. Basically, it is a great research tool that helps to provide you with the information you need.

http://candlesticker.com

This is a great free tool that you can work out the candlestick patterns you have learned in the chapters before. Evidently, this is a great source to analyze the overall success of a certain company's opening and closing stock.

Some of the most common tools you will need for penny stock investing, and should certainly be something to add to your toolkit, include:

Stock screeners. These can scan the entire market and give information on the average trading volume that is taking place, chart patterns, etc.

Charting software. This shows the performance of a stock, fund, or index over time.

Stock simulators. Ideal especially for beginners, this is a platform you can use to practice fundamental analysis or even test out trading strategies without having to necessarily spend the money. You can also work on the simulations during your actual trading process, especially to test out new strategies that you may have developed or the ideas of others, to see how it works out. Keep in mind that the simulation removes the emotional element and doesn't manage to take all the costs.

Trading newsletters. These are email or print messages that normally inform traders of unusual market movements, new developments, and innovations. Keeping up-to-date is critical in the investment world, especially when predicting the overall success that may occur. It also provides expert opinions on how stocks will hopefully move in the future and what stocks have the most potential. Now, extra work may need to be acquired to find the experts' opinions on penny stocks.

Criteria for Evaluating Stock Research Tools

- Finviz stock screener
- Moomoo
- Stock Rover
- Yewno | Edge
- Motley Fool Stock Advisor
- Benzinga Pro
- MacroRisk Analytics
- https://www.benzinga.com/money/stock-research-tools/

Best Brokers for Penny Stock Trading Links

- Fidelity - $0 per trade
- TD Ameritrade - $6.95 per OTCBB trade
- Charles Schwab - $0 per trade
- TradeStation - $0 per trade
- Interactive Brokers - $.0035 per share

Chapter 6:
Building Your Strategy

So how exactly do you go about making a strategy? This is a good question and certainly deserves a detailed answer. Research is the first ingredient to a good trade; the next would be a well-thought-out plan. As the saying goes, failing to plan is planning to fail. A strategy is a detailed and logical plan, after all, and it is best to understand the steps you can take as a beginner to formulate one that can hopefully get you a good profit.

Before You Start

Before you start with real-life trading, it is best to practice paper trading. There are a few steps you can undertake here when practicing, as you do need a few steps and rules when starting off. Besides, it is an easy as well as a realistic method for you to learn the ins and outs of trading without having to spend a dime. In all honesty, there is no disadvantage to a paper trade that can weigh down the advantages that a simulation truly brings to the table. Especially considering it can help prepare you and wrinkle out many mistakes without having suffered major losses like many people who directly start with trading certainly will suffer.

When you start your paper trade, it is best to both choose as well as write or type (if that is more your thing) your objectives. You are not just trading and risking your money to have fun; you have goals. And in order to remember and stick to them within a specific time frame, it requires you to write them down and remember them. The biggest lie you can tell anyone is that you do not need to write them down because you will remember them, which is highly doubtful. Furthermore, if you are not clear of the path you want to take, jotting down where you would like to go and what you would like to accomplish can truly narrow the path for you and give you a better idea of your objectives. Setting down the objectives for penny stock trading will make a huge difference, so don't hesitate to bring that pen and notepad with you, or even a tablet. Whatever floats your boat!

Then you will need to choose your favorite forms or types of penny stocks. It is best to have familiarized yourself with the markets you want to trade upon and choose a niche you are interested in and motivated to work in. It is wise to know the price range of the shares and the industry groups you do enjoy. Remember to set any other parameter you may have found to be important when looking up those specific penny stock markets.

Then you should decide the steps you will take when it comes to research, monitoring, and the trading of shares. It will certainly be quite exciting when you start off, but you need to know where you will begin. Which websites do you trust? Will you directly call the company? What reports do you intend to read through? Do you understand all the information that is available? Would you rather get professional help and opinions? What information sources will provide you with the best details that you need at the end of the day?

The next step would certainly be deciding on a broker unless you already have one. This is evident once you are confident with the paper trading, and all the practice you have is now ready to take the next big step. Be sure to pick a good and reliable stockbroker that is tailored to your specific needs.

There you go! Seven steps and ideas you can follow when you start with penny stocks. Not so complicated after all, but it will take a good amount of time and effort to put together. But once you get the ball rolling, things should certainly be moving at a much faster pace.

Once you are ready to start finding penny stocks to trade, here are a few things you need to consider doing:

First, research the company. This is a no-brainer, as being an informed trader means you are a smart trader. The best way to start this off is by doing a quick Google search, but this will most certainly not provide you all the answers you need. It can help you filter through the worst of the stocks, though, and determine whether the stock in question is worth spending more time on to research.

Do pay attention to the news tabs on Google search, as this is a commonly ignored feature but important and likely even useful when it comes to researching stocks. Considering there are more informative news articles than blog posts regarding the stock in question.

You will then want to look at the volatility in question. When it comes to penny stocks, it may seem ironic, but you are not looking for non-volatile stocks. Instead, you want to work with stocks that are spiking at quite a rapid pace. These are the stocks that normally have the most activity, and therefore the most promise to gain a profit (but also a loss). In these modern times, you will have more than enough software to be able to help filter the penny stocks that you are looking for. If you struggle to understand why, think of it this way: the less volatility that occurs in a trade, the fewer buyers and sellers there are when it comes to penny stocks. This means you may have quite a lot of trouble with selling your shares and overall liquidity.

Volatility in penny stocks is good and can push you way ahead of the curve when it comes to penny stock investing.

The next item you want to look for is the volume that is in the trade. Volatility is not the only factor that can determine whether a stock is a good choice or not, but it does help. No matter how promising a company appears to be, if it does not have a lot of volumes, then do not consider even trading it.

Trading volumes that run under 200,000 shares a day is pushing it, and if you want to play it safe, go with stocks that trade under 500,000 shares a day. High-volume is a sign of a large amount of interest that exists in the stocks. That means if you decide to sell, you will not have many struggles to find a buyer and that the level of liquidity that exists in that company will not or should not be difficult.

Next, you will want to look at the catalysts. Catalysts normally act as a predictor of a major event that is occurring, specifically news that can have or move a stock price regardless of whether it would be a good or bad move.

For example, if a company is about to release a brand new and exciting project, you will find it on the catalyst and possibly predict for it to have a positive impact on the company, if the product is successful, that is.

Whenever you are considering a stock, it is best to take a sneak peek at the catalyst and watch how exactly they are making the stocks move. You may even build a better idea of what to watch out for and get the hang of the trends that impact stocks.

It is good to hear the opinions of others. It does not mean you should always listen to their advice but understanding the thoughts and perspective of others can help you give that extra edge. This advice does come with a warning: it is a good idea to check what people say about penny stocks, even on social media, but always take it with a grain of salt. This should merely be a form of research and should not have any sway on your ultimate and final decision unless proven by other facts and actual reliable sources. However, at the end of the day, it is truly best to learn to think for yourself. This starts off by observing the actions of others and deducting yourself whether their moves are accurate. You aren't merely copying what they are doing but learning how to apply certain circumstances in your own favor while discarding the choices of others that will not work in your scenario.

History also has a knack for repeating itself, but never exactly to the letter, much like experiencing déjà vu. However, learning the patterns of penny stocks can give you a relatively good idea about how certain penny stocks may work out. It might be recommended to trade based on the same key patterns that occur time and again. It may seem a little boring, but it is quite reliable. And as a beginner, you need to consider applying this strategy until you get comfortable with other forms of strategies or simply stick with it if it works. That is entirely up to you.

When it comes to trading, you need to consider the time of day. In a busy life, it is quite possible to lose track of time. But when it comes to trading, it is important to keep track of what is happening. And if you have another job, it is best to adopt a trading schedule that works around yours. If you are a student, for example, then you can study and attend classes in the mornings and focus on trading in the afternoon, or even vice versa if it suits your schedule better.

The time of day you happen to work on trading can certainly change the strategy you want to take on. For instance, certain stocks are great for working on during the morning but can come up at a total loss when the day closes. This is where picking up patterns can come in handy to adapt them to your time and availability.

Avoid companies that have massive loads of debt. Any company that is in debt is a massive red flag waving from a high tower. So when you check out a penny stock company, it is important to understand all the aspects of the business, and this most definitely includes the overall financial health of a company.

To determine this, it is best to rely on the technical form of analysis but keep in account the fundamental accounts too. Take your time to read the reports to have a proper grasp of what is happening inside of the company. This is normally a good indicator of the company's health, and if you see the business is drowning in debt, it is not likely to be successful. Does this mean you cannot trade? Well, you can, but you would have to adjust the strategy and keep in mind that the debts will play a massive factor on the stocks. As a result, you are at a higher risk of running at a loss.

You would want to keep an eye out for penny stocks that do have higher and more favorable ratios in their liquidity. Every company has its fair share of assets and debts, and when you compare the two, this will reveal the liquidity ratio. If the company has a higher ratio in assets than debt, then it is more ideal because it is a key indicator that the capital of the business outweighs the debt. This means the company is functioning quite well at this point in time and holds promise for action in the future.

Next, you will need to consider using a stock screener, as this will help to narrow down the choices you make based on the criteria you have set down. In addition, it can allow you to search a larger number of factors, volume, volatility, etc.

Tips to Develop A Penny Stock Strategy

First, you need to have a healthy respect for the risk involved. This is likely to develop over time, but don't ever ignore it. Don't fear it either though, just have respect for it. Wherever you can, work on avoiding the risk. It is just overall better in the long run.

Be clear on the goals you have. Be crystal clear because the better idea you have about what you want, the easier it is to come up with a concise plan.

As a beginner, it is recommended to start small. No matter how keen you may be or what you have indeed learned, starting small and building your way up reduces a lot of risk and cushions your losses when they do come from time to time. Furthermore, starting small, especially at the beginning, curbs any massive problems or debt by completely avoiding them in the first place.

Another great tip to shorten your learning curve is by choosing a mentor. You specifically would want a mentor who has indeed walked the same path as you hope to. The mentor can help by preventing many of the mistakes you could make and hiding you too different strategies you may not have considered. Again, it is wise to learn to think for yourself, but no one said that you weren't allowed any form of help after all.

Do not take an extra risk by forcing a trade just because you feel like a trade should happen. If you need to force a trade, it means you are doing something wrong or perhaps a little hastily. Rather, wait for the trade to come to you, and do not make any decisions about a trade that thoroughly diverges from your original trading plan without a solid and verified reason.

Things to Look For in Stocks While Day Trading

When you are working with penny stocks, it is known to be more of a hands-on approach. This means that you are going to have to learn the craft of day trading in order to take advantage of the more volatile market that runs throughout the day.

Here are some things to keep an eye out for when you start off and progress in day trading as a penny stock trader. These are tips to find the potentially hottest trade that runs on that day:

First, it is a catalyst. News happens to be one of the primary causes of stocks to move upwards or downwards at a rapid pace. That is why it is so important to stay updated on the trends and news without having that bias, but if you can predict a trend, then you can also find yourself ahead of the curve, which is the ideal scenario.

You also want to keep an eye out for a low float stock. This is where insiders and actual major investors do tend to have ownership of most of the shares. This means there is a limited number of stocks, and the shareholders are quite limited to selling. This ultimately means that the demand and supply work well, and a lot of price fluctuations will be occurring there.

It is obviously ideal if you can spot a killer chart pattern. This is when you discover a pattern that has a promising trend to use for your benefit. Therefore, it is so incredibly important to learn chart patterns, as your day trading will benefit from your understanding of patterns and chart readings.

Evidently, you also want to look for signs of the increased trading volume. This is when you see a rise in shares being traded over quite a short period of time. This is normally a big indicator of hype over a specific stock and trader piling in to get their load of some good profits.

Key Terms to Know as a Beginner

Trading has its own language, and it is important to know what people are talking about. However, you will discover that learning the language yourself is not too complicated, and here are a few terms you do need to be aware of as you kickstart your day trading:

Long: Long stock normally means you usually own stock where you earn money if the price rises and lose money if the price lowers.

Short: This occurs when you borrow a stock and sell it on the market. You are then under a certain obligation to purchase the stock back and even go on returning it. You profit with the vice versa strategy, where you earn a profit if the price falls and come up at a loss if the price rises.

NYSE: New York Stock Exchange, which happens to be one of the largest exchanges in the world. Multiple of the world's largest companies are traded on this platform, and therefore NYSE is a massive and popular platform for traders on a global scale.

Support: The support level that appears on a chart is when a clear level of market or security happens to drop in its history. For example, if a certain stock reached seven dollars and they bounced down several times, then seven dollars would be the official support level.

Resistance: The exact opposite to the support level, where a level at a specific market has dropped in the past before bouncing back up. If a stock declines and stops at seven dollars before rising again, then seven dollars would be the official resistance level of the penny stock you are investigating.

The Official Step-By-Step Guide on How to Trade Penny Stocks

When you are reading about a penny stock, you are under a higher risk than the actual trade. The risk is multiplied when you add pink sheets and OTC exchanges instead of the traditional NYSE and NASDAQ exchanges.

That is why it is crucial to have strict and serious criteria under which the penny stock will fall, and it is why you want to practice matters such as risk management.

One idea is that you can focus on day trading penny stock. As you may have seen mentioned time and again, penny stocks are far more suited for the short-term game, and normal stocks are certainly suited better for the last.

Another popular step for risk management in trading is not to hold your stocks overnight, where the most the same can be done without you knowing.

Now the first step you can take with day trading is by trading only the best and simply leaving the rest behind. It is a simple concept that falls under the idea that you must have strict criteria. You can use a stock scanner, which can make your life so much easier for you and cut a lot of the work time you have on figuring out trades in half, if not more.

Each morning, you can start off by listing the stocks that fit under the criteria in which you will trade.

The second step is to trade the best quality setups. The first step is trading with the best stocks. Now, you want to be able to trade with the best setups, such as bull flags or even flat top breakout patterns.

These are the chart patterns most professional traders simply trade, considering they are at the lowest level of risk, and they also share many similar characteristics. They normally both require stocks to make some big moves up, then a quick pullback that happens to have a sell-off. If you ever find yourself in doubt, consider asking and finding out whether the stock you are selling has a once-a-year type of event that occurs. This is normally the ideal time to jump in and trade with this stock. Normally you can identify a bull flag when you see the candlestick on the sales of trade, making a new high right after the pullback has indeed occurred.

The next step is to join a community of traders in a chat room if possible. In order to be one of the best traders, it is certainly helpful to surround yourself with the best. There is a lot you will be able to learn from them, as well as a supportive community that can help you with your trades, problems, and even mental tricks. Don't follow a trader's advice blindly, but as a beginner, you are certainly allow yourself to learn more from people who have practiced the art of trading for years. Although, be sure that the chat room you join for traders has professionals, and be aware of scammers as online communities are famous for misbranding. However, a big positive benefit is the likelihood of having a community that informs others of a trade that shows great potential. The likelihood of a good trade getting spotted is infinitely higher and can be a great advantage as well. Not only do you learn from them, but a community's knowledge and like-minded goals can have you reaping profits you may have never reached on your own.

At the end of the day, you may find the repetitive patterns to be quite boring, but sometimes repetition is necessary. There is not a massive secret ingredient or recipe to becoming a multimillionaire in trading. But learning from the best, following what works, and sticking to the rules can certainly pay off in the long run.

Chapter 7:
Research & Analyze: Tips and Tricks

You certainly would have heard time and again that the key to trading is research. There is no doubt that knowledge is power and is critical when it comes to the decisions you need to make. But how exactly do you do research on a topic that has little information? Where do you need to look, and why do you need to look for this info? There are certain steps you will need to take in order to gain more confidence in analyzing penny stocks and ensure they are getting the best returns.

How to Get Information About Microcap/Penny Stock Companies?

This is a tricky question, as one of the disadvantages is the level of difficulty to retrieve information on the penny stock. However, just because it may be difficult does not mean it is altogether impossible, and there are certainly a few things you could do in order to get the information you need. Keep in mind that if you struggle with information or nothing pans out about a certain penny stock, then you do need to steer clear. The less information that is shared, the more likely it could be a scam. Transparency is certainly a thing to be desired when searching for a good company to invest in.

Firstly, it is best to ask the company whether it is indeed registered with the SEC and if it files the necessary reports to the SEC. Suppose a company is small enough not to have to comply with this. In that case, you can also consider calling your state regulators in order to get the information you need, as well as the company management and brokers who have recommended for you to invest in the company. If you already know anyone who has invested in the company, ask them how it has been faring. But remember to be cautious and wise with the information you receive. You need to consider whether the management has the proper experience to execute the business plan it advertises. This means you should have a good knowledge of how a business should be run. This may seem obvious, but most people do not have that piece of common knowledge. You may need to consider whether the company also has the proper resources or any form of competitive advantage that show any good signs of succeeding. Finally, be careful when reviewing the company's website. Even checking out the quality and design of it can certainly be a good indicator of how up-to-date it is with the digital world. You can also contemplate searching for information on the company on the OTC market websites.

You can find information from the SEC, as many companies are required to file their reports with the

SEC. This means you can use the SEC's EDGAR database to discover which company files at the SEC itself (so if you do not get a hold of management, you can always check there), and you can receive the reports that the company has sent in to file. However, if a company does file their reports to the SEC but does not place them on EDGAR, you can reach out to the SEC's online form or email the public information office to find out the information you need.

You can also look up the information at your state securities regulator. This is especially valid if you have difficulty finding the information of the microcap company directly from the company, your broker, or even the SEC. As you can see, you do have a few options and sources to find out the information you would like. When you contact the state securities regulator, you can check to make sure whether the company has been legally cleared and allowed to sell securities in your state. This is a sure-fire way to avoid most of the scams and cons out there, as most traders will not go so far with their effort to discover the information necessary. But laziness comes at a price, and so does knowledge. So take your time to make sure you are confident in the company before bringing any sort of money even close to them.

You can check from other government regulators as well. For example, many companies do not have to file reports to the SEC, such as certain banks. However, the banks or companies do need to have filed updated financial information at their own banking regulators. And many of the regulators are quite easy to access online. Therefore, you can discover what you need in the comfort of your own home.

Another common source of information is reference books, websites, and even commercial databases. It may not be a bad idea to pay a visit to your local public library or the nearest business or law school library. You will find many referencing materials that happen to contain information you may need about companies, especially the company you will be interested in. In addition, you can access commercial databases, which may have far more history about a company's history, products and services, management, revenues, and even go as far as the credit ratings, which is critical to see how a company handles its debt. Again, occasionally doing proper research requires going the extra mile. This is certainly a wise example, but better to get the needed details than regret it with a massive loss later. Considering that the SEC cannot endorse or recommend any form of business, using the commercial database gives room for consultation and possibly a more expert opinion on how the companies are faring. Being unbiased is demanded by law for the SEC, so as a beginner, despite getting the necessary reports, it may be wise to start consulting with professionals in the commercial database.

You can also consider going to the secretary of state, where the company is specifically incorporated. Contacting the Secretary of State is a good way to find out whether the company is in good standing. It might even be possible for you to receive copies of the incorporating papers as well as annual reports of the company you are indeed interested in. These are all good sources to consider for penny stock companies but do keep in mind that just because companies do have the appearance of readily available information or file reports does not altogether mean it is safe to invest in. Check out the reports and be careful with your investment decision. It is still a possibility that a company is perfectly legal and can still fail, or the company is good at masking its true intentions. Again, this all brings about the element of risk. That is why it is so important to practice caution and why you will be reminded of this repeatedly throughout the course of this book.

How to Pick Penny Stock Winners Pre-Strike

What should be the determining factors for choosing a penny/microcap company? There are certain rules you can follow and keep in mind when it comes to a penny stock.

Look for the stocks that you can see are already spiking. One of the fastest ways of identifying this is by finding a stock that is already moving. This can normally be seen through charts and other forms of analysis. Keep in mind that due to information inefficiencies, it might be difficult to catch it from the beginning, but it does not mean you can't hop along while it is still a part of the move.

Keep an eye out for any potential breakouts that may reach new highs. Looking for a stock that can reach new highs, especially during the day, is a rewarding strategy to be aware of. For example, if you see that it is indeed a Friday afternoon and the stock is still holding the same high as in the morning, there is always the potential for a short squeeze before the market closes. For a penny stock trader, a short squeeze is most definitely something you need to learn to recognize in the marketing world, as it can be rewarding for you in the long run. This is because when potential breakouts do happen to reach the new highs, they will not be able to keep the price in their previous resistance level, and in the end, you will be earning greater profits than even possibly planned.

Another rule of thumb to follow through on is always betting the price on the action. The price action basically gives you a real story about what is happening with the stock. Companies may lie, but numbers and figures don't. You can figure out whether a stock is breaking a new high or starting a downward trend, even if the news sites in the entire world give no indication of what is occurring. The stock charts are an important and relevant tool of information for you to use at your full capacity.

Take your time to watch price movements. If anything, it will be educational, and although it might be quite tiresome, this is the best way to catch on to patterns that you certainly will not have noticed on otherwise. Make it interesting by turning it into a game. Place bets for yourself on which stock price you believe in moving next. If you are wrong, figure out why, and if you are right, feel free to reward yourself with a good cup of coffee or tea. You certainly did earn it!

Once you start gaining more confidence in your betting game, you can consider placing money into your predictions, or if you still don't feel too confident, paper trade and build your way up until you work with actual money. Keep in mind that sometimes, you still are going to bet wrong, but it is best to learn from it and move on.

Next, do your research. This is no surprise to you, but this is one of the most common reasons traders fail. Laziness is a terrible word to use, but unfortunately, it is a reality in many investors' lives. People like to trust what others tell them instead of doing the grunt work themselves. But grunt work does pay off, and in the end, you will see yourself far more rewarded than those who attempted to wing it with the bare minimum of information.

When knowing the best penny stocks you need to buy, consider the following: remember former runners, hot sectors, sympathy plays, and news. They all play a role in penny stocks and should be something you will actively keep tabs on. It may seem like a lot of extra work, but it is entirely necessary to stay sharp and much ahead of the game as needed. Success does require a lot of hard work as well as determination and grit. Success requires you to go over and beyond what most people are not willing to do. It may not be fun, but it is necessary.

Consider this: If you are willing to take just another half hour on learning all that you can about penny stocks as well as the company, then you are way more informed than the majority of traders. That gives you leverage and an edge that most other people don't have.

Another aspect is to think like a retired trader. You only make a move if you must. You are not going into retirement, but thinking in this mindset can help you maneuver against the pent-up emotional plays that tend to string along countless other traders. People who have a "retired" mindset will not come out of retirement for a trade that is barely valuable, if it is worth anything at all. Do not waste your time on so-so traders. You are not shooting for a minor league; you are working for the best trades.

Selecting A Penny Stockbroker

Choosing the right broker for the job is a good tip for success again. The top penny brokers do charge reasonable fees, but they are also quite supportive and tend to be far more friendly. So there are certainly a lot of qualities you will need to consider when choosing a penny stockbroker. But just like choosing penny stock, you will need to do the same amount of research on a stockbroker to make sure you know what they offer and whether you can sufficiently trust them.

Consider whether the stockbroker has an online or even possible mobile trading platform. Determine whether you could have access to the online or even mobile version of a broker's app. Using this method, you can know whether a trade is going against you or for you wherever you are.

It is also best to check out the minimum deposit. Although many online brokers do not require this, it is always best to completely make sure. You will obviously want to have a fund regardless of the deposit fee or not.

Supply & Demand and Tape Reading

So, where do supply and demand come into play with stocks, and what on earth does tape reading mean? Well, a tape can be considered as a brief summary of all the trades that had occurred during the day. It shows people the price, size, and time of the trade made individually. It is a good strategy many penny-stock traders use to analyze the movers that occur throughout the day as well as seeing and identifying the fluctuations and potential opportunities that occur.

When a trade is executed, it is normally called a print, which is the total number of shares that had been both bought and sold. It is the price at which the share had indeed been sold, as well as the time at which the trade happened to take place.

For most trades, they occur at the asking price, which happens to be in green color. If the trade does, however, occur at a bid price, it will be in red, and if the trade happens literally between the two, then a person can see it in white. This might not mean anything of too much importance, but it is good not to make any false assumptions about the information and specifically its color codes, as red is normally understood in a negative light, especially in the financial world.

One of the ways you can use this to your advantage is by picking up the specific patterns of the trade that is occurring. For example, you can pick up the speed at which the shares are moving, as well as the volume and the offers and bids that are being held.

Short Sale Restrictions (SSR)

This is a short-selling strategy you can consider but is not normally recommended. However, it is always good to know how it works. For example, if the stock happens to decline at 10% or even more from the close of the previous day, the SSR will basically be set in motion to restrict the amount of trading occurring with that stock until the end of the next trading day.

This rule does apply to any stock, no matter where they are traded, but this rule can have a massive impact on penny stock traders. Any declines of more than 10% could work as a great advantage in day trading, but this then gets heavily manipulated in the restriction that had been placed a decade ago. It is advised not to practice short selling, but if you are considering it, then please be advised that the restrictions will act as a major disadvantage when trying out this strategy. You may struggle to make a profit with this one.

Technical and Fundamental Analysis

You will have to practice both fundamental and technical analysis when it comes to the specific stocks that you will want to buy. So, for example, although you may not necessarily be looking at penny stocks when it comes to the long term, it doesn't mean they are exempt for the same amount of analysis as you would when it comes to other stocks.

Fundamental analysis occurs when you look at the company itself, specifically its earnings, the economy, and the financials that are happening within the company, as well as keeping an eye on the information that is related to the specific company itself. This is a bigger and more important factor when you are strategizing for the long haul. However, it is still a good practice to be aware of what is going on in the company when taking on penny stocks. You might not have to focus so intensively on the long-term future.

Technical analysis has more to do with the stock charts, the data that is trending, as well as any other technical factors that have to do with the company's financial performance, specifically regarding its shares. This is a critical skill you will have to learn when it comes to trading penny stocks, and important that you understand the full scope before diving into penny stock investing.

Scanning for Stocks to Trade

There are thousands of strategies in the world that you can find and use when you are trading penny stocks, but they will not all work for you and your circumstances, nor the company that you are interested in investing in. Therefore, it is important to practice in a simulation to see what you are comfortable with and, just in general, to help you figure out what exactly you are doing. There are a few rules that you can focus on following to help you out: First, you can focus on doing some pre-market research. This is where you will find stocks that work with your specific criteria before the market even opens for that specific day.

Second, it is important to look for "gappers," which is when something big is happening in the company, like massive news that has been released. A stock that happens to be gapping is when it fits all good criteria points for trading but is at a lower point than you thought it might be.

Third, you will need to have a good understanding of chart patterns. This is where math in school paid off, as you will now have to learn to read them carefully. Many strategies are reliant on the analysis of the candlestick chart, and it is best to identify when they are having an upward or downward trend.

This is speculative data, and a lot of deductions need to be made. However, if you practice these methods correctly, you can make quite strong and potentially accurate instructions for the long hall. This is especially helpful if you spot items such as a bull flag pattern. This normally defines items such as risk points and is a great indicator of when you need to pull out of a specific trade.

It is important for you to get comfortable with speculation as penny stock trading focuses more on having a good grasp on behavioral aspects and the picking up of patterns.

Avoiding Scams

Apart from common rookie mistakes, scams and fraud are most likely to be one of the most common forms of downfalls that do occur for a trader. However, the likelihood of recovering losses from scams is small, and it is just best to normally avoid them altogether. Here are the top tips to keeping yourself safe and avoiding these scams when it comes to trading:

Firstly, consider every penny stock recommendation as a scam until it is proven otherwise. Next, you need to look for the source of the report and make sure you understand where the information of the business and stocks come from. Recommendations could so easily be made from paid promoters or insiders of a company. Check and double-check!

Secondly, steps have been given for you to properly investigate a company. Consider the rule, "Investigate before investing." This will save you a lot of pain and trouble in the long run. Be careful when you read their financial statements and any other forms of information you may get a hold of. The more information you gather, all the better, as again, the more transparent a company is, the less likely it is to be a scam. After all, legal companies normally have nothing to hide, but scammers have so much to keep in the dark. If you cannot find out enough information about the company, then play it safe and don't invest. You need to have a good amount of confidence to even consider placing your money into an investment.

It is also good to look for the exchange. Finding penny stocks on some of the major exchanges is always a good sign. If you find them on OTC or pink sheets, it means they normally don't meet listing requirements on the major exchanges and are likely to be a higher risk.

If you can, do your best to verify any claims they do make. Those who promote penny stock tend to make lucrative claims such as a potential massive release or a promise of the gold mine or a bucket of gold at the end of the rainbow. Basically, they will lie. That is a fact. It is best to discern which company is telling the truth and which ones are grasping on desperate marketing tactics. Do not fall for the bait as many people do. This will again only get you into massive trouble. Be sure that the companies' claims are backed up by legitimate sources.

Always be skeptical rather than gullible. There is no such thing as a quick-rich scheme. Those who managed to get rich quickly are purely through a stroke of luck, nothing more. Follow the rule: "If it is too good to be true, then it more than likely is."

Playing it safe than sorry is generally the better rule of thumb to follow.

If you are investing and trading online, it is also best to take extra precautions when you are working on your computer, tablet, or smartphone. Basically, any device that has an internet connection does happen to be vulnerable to hackers. So when you are working with money online, it is certainly best to ramp up the level of security that runs on your devices. You should definitely consider getting a VPN so that no one can track you or your movements online. This may not seem too important as an investor, but online security is the same as taking your money and valuables to a safe.

Be careful of the messages you receive, especially phone calls. If you receive phone calls from a company out of the blue, then alarm bells already need to be going off, considering that most companies do not call unless they are a scam. Also, double-check any links that are sent to you and be aware of phishing sites that might look almost identical to the original website.

Basically, practice extra caution, and if something seems off to you, then steer further away.

Additional Tips for Research

Avoiding scams, looking up companies, and making sure you are a step ahead are all important tips. There are, however, some additional tips you can follow through on to help improve your overall chances of success as a trader.

You can start off by checking the SEC website for the stock listing status. It is a good idea to know where a company stands with the SEC, regardless of what information you may have garnered directly from the company itself.

You can also focus on getting copies of the company's most recent SEC filings from a fee online financial provider. Again, it means free information that gives you a nudge ahead in the right direction.

You also need to take a step into your business shoes by figuring out how exactly the company is making money and how much it stands to make using the financial report. This is best to determine and verify any claims that they do make, as well as see if they are running as they should. In general, it is a great way to see the raw and truthful potential of a business. It may be time to brush up on a little accounting as you sneak a peek into the financial world of the business you take an interest in investing in.

Finally, you can pick a penny stock that is trending with a minimum volume of 100,000 shares. This is a good rule of thumb when finding good penny stocks.

All in all, there are many tactics and strategies you can find. But at the end of the day, a lot of these matters are based on the decisions regarding your specific circumstances and budget. You need to work out whether the risk is worth the reward, whether the companies pan out, and whether you are following through on a great strategy. Be careful with every choice you make, but if you do make a mistake, learn from it, and don't beat yourself up about it because everyone makes them. Being a savvy investor means you won't give up but rather that you'll try again. It is a game of logic, after all, and though you may have lost in one move, you certainly can plan how to strike on the next.

Chapter 8:
Effective Trading Strategies

You are not alone when forming a strategy. In fact, there are many strategies available for you to use as you kick-start your investing journey. It would be wise to start with them first before developing your own strategies, as this can give a more practical idea about the trading world without having to create a plan from scratch. Building experience is equally important as designing a strategy, as they normally work hand in hand.

Scanning, Searching, And Striking

There are three rules you need to follow with one of the trading strategies. These are good steps to follow, especially as a beginner:

The first step is scanning. You can use a stock scanner to find penny stocks that fit into a certain category; basically, the best penny stocks that have the highest potential for success.

You would want a market cap that falls safely between $50 million and $300 million. You will also want the target price to be 5% above price and the current volume to be above $1 million. It is preferable to target penny stocks in the US and purchase shares that are under $5. On technical matters, it is best to focus on the price to be above $200 a day as a simple moving average.

The second step involves searching. You will have to filter between the results that scans have revealed, looking through the watch list of filtered stocks to find the best pattern. You will want to find the stocks that have the clearest price action. These penny stocks have the highest potential and should be considered seriously after doing the necessary research on the companies, as well as analyzing their success. Do not leave it merely up to a scanner to tell you whether you should invest in this specific group. It only helps you narrow down your options, but it is important to verify whether an investment choice is good because artificial intelligence focuses on statistics, not reason.

Then, once you have found the stock you are interested in, it is certainly time to strike and hold on to the stock until you wait for the pattern to be confirmed.

Trade Penny Stocks That May Interest You

Another option is specifically selecting companies that you are interested in and sticking out for you specifically. Then, do the necessary research, making sure it is extensive, and consider all the external factors. External factors are items such as an economic outlook and geopolitical climates.

Remember to use limit orders. This can certainly help to limit your losses and works when predicting the stock's trends. Limit orders should also help to buy and sell at the prices you can benefit from, with you having to constantly monitor your stocks 24/7.

Tier trading occurs when you split up the initial capital and purchase stocks at different tiers. For example, you can start with a smaller starter position in order to validate the trading thesis. The moment your stock increases, then you add a second tier.

Top Patterns to Know When Penny Stock Trading

Every trader has their own personal traders when they are trading. As a result, Penny stock trading has a lot of technical analysis involved rather than fundamental analysis.

Penny stock technical analysis tends to work with chart patterns as well as indicators. So the best way to learn how to work with them is through paper trading.

Support and Resistance Lines

Support and resistance lines happen to be important for any trader. They point out all the points of strengths and weaknesses a company has undergone. This is vital because it shows traders the best time to enter and leave stocks. Basically, patterns emerge, and identifying them will allow you to increase your chances of profiting, learning when to buy and sell. That is ideal, especially for a volatile platform, where it is best to know when to leave and when to climb onboard.

Support lines are normally drawn when a stock bounces at a specific price—for example, one dollar. If the stock happens to approach one dollar again, traders will start to bounce off and move upward. The same could be said if the stock has a two-dollar resistance line, as this normally means the stock will have an incredibly difficult time breaking the two dollars.

When you use the support and resistance lines in trading, you will need to understand that when the support is broken, it becomes resistance, and when the resistance is broken, it becomes the support.

Bull Flag

This is another common penny stock chart pattern. In this matter, it is important to see the consolidation and continuation. Bull flag patterns only occur when there is generally a strong move upwards and have shaped about 1-3 candles.

Whenever there is a significant movement in price, the volume must be present. If a bull flag does happen to form on little volume, it means that it is difficult for the stock to break out. A breakout only occurs when a seller finally steps in. Basically, it does not have a high rate of liquidity if it struggles with volume.

Double Bottom

This penny stock chart pattern is the reversal of a continuation pattern and can be just as beneficial for investors. The double bottom pattern happens when the price of a stock reaches the same low price twice but then pushes itself back up. This normally gives the chart a "W" shape. It also means the business can recover from losses and has done so before. It is generally ideal for investors to jump into this when the stock is bouncing back from the second low that it has had. But it is important to keep an eye on the stock traders over the next couple of days in order to make sure it is carrying on with its uptrend. Because despite what the pattern may indicate, there is still a level of unpredictability, and it is wise to remain cautious despite what the chart might be revealing.

Golden Cross Chart Pattern

This is known to be quite a lagging indicator, but the golden cross does happen to be one of the most sought-after patterns when it comes to trading. A lagging indicator normally confirms certain trends are taking place and not predicting them. This is because the chart uses a past price action instead of the currency action that is taking place. Normally a golden cross happens to occur when the 50-day happens to be a simple moving average across the 200-day moving average.

This is normally considered to be a bullish sign for a strong upwards trend. Traders normally use this golden cross form if they are in it for more long-term trades. Seasoned traders also use indicators other than the golden cross to fully confirm their decisions when they are buying penny stocks. It is the mark of a savvy investor to always double-check the information given. It would be wise if you adopted the same trend and form of thinking. Never take something at direct face value, even if it happens to be coming from a chart.

Fibonacci Retracement

This is a trading strategy that is quite a bit more complex than those covered before. Normally it should be used in line with other chart patterns such as the bullish flag, a way to confirm or verify a specific trend. This is a good chart to use as a day trader, and you normally draw the chart from the previous day's close to the high of the day.

All these strategies and tools can be considered as a stepping stone and a helping hand when you first start trading. You can even consider using them as an experienced trader if you find levels of success and profits in them. Work on sticking to the plans and rules and be careful not to get emotionally attached. The best way to start, including reading the charts and picking up the patterns, is by using the simulators that are readily available for you to use.

A good strategy is critical for your success and is certainly a carved path for you as a beginner. Keep these strategies in mind, and even discover others on your own. Find out what makes the most logical sense for you. Be entirely sure that you do understand the strategy itself before following through on it. Because if you don't understand a strategy, then how on earth do you expect it to work?

Chapter 9:
Do's and Don'ts of Trading Penny Stocks

When you learn about penny stock trading, you are bound to make a couple of mistakes. But it is certainly better to avoid many of them by learning from the mistakes of others. This is by learning the certain do's and don'ts when you are working with trading penny stocks. First, you need a good understanding of some things you should never do and what you should rather consider doing instead.

Do's in Trading Penny Stocks

A rule every wise investor follows is as follows: only invest with risk money or funds that you can afford to lose. We cannot stress enough the importance of this choice and how people have fallen far by blatantly ignoring this rule. Many people have put all they have in hopes of gaining more, only to lose and struggle to get back on their feet. In short, they became far worse off than when they began, and you must absolutely avoid this. Never put in money you cannot afford to lose. Just do not do that to yourself.

It is best to keep your sights on the decisions and movements of experts in trading. Many of them are quite public with their decisions, educating others with what they have learned. It is best to keep an eye on them, as they are far more likely to pick up problems more efficiently than you could on your own. It does not mean to follow them blindly and question their decisions in order to understand their logic and build your own, but it is certainly a trick to success to learn from the best.

Start paper trading, as this is the simulation that has been mentioned before—a great way to practice your craft without necessarily risking your money. Most expert traders still use paper simulations to test out their new strategies. It just makes sense. If you have a field to practice in, then why not take advantage of it? You will be taking some time and learning in an environment that is far more friendly than real life. Now, it takes that emotional element away, and you can only practice such matters in the real trading world. But it certainly helps you to prepare. And it is no surprise that those who use paper trading have higher chances of being successful than those who jump into it blindly. You are far likely to suffer fewer losses simply by testing out your strategies on a platform that can give you an idea of whether your plans are flawed or practical.

Buy what you know. If you do not understand your market, how on earth are you supposed to pick up when a business is doing well or making a sharp incline for the worst? If you cannot understand whether the business is staying ahead of the competition or merely in one place, then failure is right at your doorstep.

It is best to be passionate about what you are investing in. This can act as a greater motivating factor to do your research, as well as have a greater understanding of the industry. For example, suppose you are interested in cycling. In that case, investing in businesses with cycling trails may be quite practical as you will understand what bikers enjoy and whether the business is running as it should be or has the potential for growth. On the other hand, you will not have the same idea when it comes to a fishing business if you do not take any interest in fishing. If you do not understand a specific business, then you should do enough research and studies on it until you are confident enough before investing. This can save you from making blind decisions.

Remember to set goals. If you have no pathway you want to follow, then again, you will be stumbling around with no good purpose. You need to set for yourself SMART goals and make sure they are practical for your lifestyle and budget. You also need to learn to stick to your goals as far as possible and only change them if absolutely need be or to greatly improve your success after you learn a particular goal may not have been so practical, as that is also a possibility.

Try out different sources for investment picks. Again, this is diversifying your investments, giving a cushion for a business to fail, or gaining success on one business while the other merely trudges along. As a penny stock investor, it is a lot easier to diversify your portfolio as well as the different markets, considering it is far more achievable.

However, pick specific industries to focus on, so although you can have a variety of businesses you are interested in, make sure they all fall into similar niches. This can give you space and room to master the knowledge you need of that niche. Otherwise, you are bringing on yourself a massive headache by picking vastly different industries, and keeping track will inevitably be a nightmare. Again, it is best to focus on a few industries rather than a vast amount.

Remember to call investor relations of each of the companies you choose. It is certainly great to get into contact with the businesses themselves. Even if you do not invest directly with them, it is not recommended. Thus, finding out directly from them the information you would like to know.

Watch and wait. Don't immediately jump into investing. Instead, take time to practice trading simulations and ensure that you are confident with your strategy. Keep an eye on the business you are interested in and keep analyzing it. Considering penny stock movements occur within days, you will not have to wait too long to understand how the business works and which direction it is currently heading in.

Always gauge the outcome of a given trade and learn from what happened. Regardless of whether it had a good and bad outcome, it is best to study and understand what went wrong or right. Being able to identify these steps can certainly help you in the future, especially in avoiding certain mistakes or jumping onto another potentially successful trade.

Remember to cut losses as quickly and as calmly as you can. If things do happen to go downhill, and you can clearly see this, it is best to jump in and cut losses as quickly as you can manage. The last thing you want is to wait things out, only to lose well beyond what you could have saved had you decided to jump in and cut your losses immediately. However, there is a delicate balance when it comes to this, as some people cut their losses too quickly and end up missing out. This is a decision you will purely need to make if the scenario does happen to arise.

Also, do not be afraid to get out of a trade when the performance doesn't match the realistic expectations you have set. If things do go slow, or have a steady decline, then it is best to leave the board again before you lose out.

Take small wins and gains in order to prevent big losses. Sometimes you may not earn as much as you want to, but it is better to win a little less than lose a lot more in the trading world. Some risks are certainly not worth taking.

Remember to be flexible for both long-term and short-term growth. Although it is good to have endurance and stick with a plan, if there arise some unexpected circumstances, adapting your plan to best respond to them is critical. Also, being flexible means staying up-to-date with the latest tools, news, technology, and even trends that tend to spring up left, right, and center within the trading world.

Keep a detailed trading diary. This is perfect for making sure you record both your successes and losses. Being able to back-track and recall your actions in the past is especially important to make sure mistakes won't be repeated and successful strategies will be used again. On the other hand, it is near impossible to remember every action you take or every decision you make. Keeping a journal is especially ideal if you want to review a trade gone wrong or right and you would like to understand the path you took that had brought you to that point.

Take on predictable gains. If it is predictable in trade, why skip out because it is predictable? This is just common sense, after all, and not a battlefield. You will want to take hold of every opportunity that is thrown your way, and if you see quite a predictable gain, don't be ashamed to go for it.

Use scanners.

Be humble and always willing to learn. This is how people succeed. If you listen to the success stories of thousands of people, you will hear many similarities spread throughout them all. Many of them, being humble about how they had gotten this far. Give credit where credit is due, and keep an open mind. This means being willing to learn from others, even if they might have less experience than you. They may have different points of view. Being humble will also allow you to be more careful with the choices you make, allowing you to avoid unnecessary mistakes that normally come at the price of being arrogant.

Be okay with starting out small. Everyone must start somewhere; and again, it is best to keep an open mind about where you can start and what you can afford. In fact, you are being kind to yourself if you approach trading with a realistic mindset and work on growing your capabilities as a trader. Keep in mind that most success stories don't happen overnight, and everyone does have to start somewhere.

Don'ts as A Penny Stock Trader

Do not simply invest in whatever is the "hottest industry." Although it is great to be aware of the trends, sometimes following the route everyone else does is a common mistake. Rather, only invest if you are confident in your plan and strategy, not just based on the speculation of others. Oftentimes, what you see when it comes to the "hottest industry" are people buying out of FOMO, where logic flies out of the window. This is especially the time to practice caution and be aware of the reason why a specific stock is trending. If you cannot see a valid reason, then stay far away because it is far more likely to burst once the illusion of a company's success is discovered.

Do not give any attention to the non-volatile as well as illiquid penny stocks. Non-volatile means they are not moving fast, sure, but it also means you are far less likely to earn something from them in the long haul.

Do not listen to your gut, especially when you are emotional. Investing drains your emotions and brings out panic or greed. Without having the firm boundaries of logic and reason in place, then you are going to fail long before you even come close to succeeding. A lot of people in movies say to follow your gut, and sure, when it comes to certain matters such as people, an emotional feeling is what you need. However, trade does not operate that way as it works on strategy, and therefore it is best to double-check every decision you make to ensure it does not ride on emotion because that is a quick ticket out of the trading business.

Do not believe in press releases or what social media tells you. News has a way of lying or telling half-truths, even when it comes to trade. So why even consider using it as a reliable source? It is best to handle any social media posts and press releases with a grain of salt. Remember, the truth can easily be twisted in any way people want it to be. It is best to discover the truth through sources other than press releases and most definitely other than social media, which can be a thriving base for scammers.

Do not be desperate for a trade. Patience is a virtue in any investor's world. It is certainly far better to wait for the trade to come to you. Although speed and proficiency are necessary for certain elements of trading, waiting is certainly another. You can consider trading to be far more of a marathon than a sprint, where time is your ally and patience is your skill.

Do not expect big gains in the beginning. Especially if you yourself have a limited budget, and you just start out trading. Having a realistic mindset on such matters can save you from a whole lot of disappointment, and you should certainly keep this in mind as a beginner to save you from making radical decisions after suffering your first loss.

Do not be afraid of taking a day off when there are no great plays. Taking a day off can be quite relieving, giving you rest and time to have a new perspective on matters. Trading is stressful, and taking a day off when you see the opportunity is certainly recommended for everyone. Being able to come back the next day refreshed and fighting will set you ahead of your competition who did not take the break.

And you should trade only if you have $50 to even $300. Certainly, any less than that will mean you are likely to suffer a loss from commission fees without getting high enough returns.

Do not buy penny stocks unless they have a great catalyst.

Although it is good to take a day off from trading, it is still best to check in on the markets every day if possible. It might add a little stress but keeping an eye on the updates is critical in fast-moving trades, especially with penny stocks.

Do not ever go all in, despite the promises and potential a penny stock trade may have, because this is not a poker game. You cannot play a bluff in hopes of fooling the market. Remember to weigh on the side of caution and be careful with where you put your resources. Going all-in on a particular stock despite its promises is a foolish move because although you have the possibility of making great gains, the pendulum can switch just as easily over to a great loss. Then you will be kicked out of the game, such as in poker, if your bluff or card loses.

Do not always believe in gurus. Keep in mind that they are making money from teaching webinars, but they will always hold something back. They will certainly not show every single trade they make either. They help others succeed to a certain degree but always keep a missing piece to themselves. It is simply the way it works for them, and you need to keep this in mind. There is always a truth or reality missing from what they may be saying to keep you behind. It is best for you to discover this truth rather yourself rather than relying completely on them. How else do you think they are going to profit from you?

10 Rules for Penny Stock Trading

1. It is best to ignore the penny-stock success stories spread via emails and social media because this may instigate people to copy their steps. The problem is that what may have worked then will probably not work now. It is best not to be influenced too much by success stories that probably did not explain everything about their process either.

2. Don't listen to tips, and do read disclaimers. Penny stocks are sold more times than they are purchased, mostly through the tips that come from newsletters or emails. The newsletters do not give you helpful tips. They are marketing for money purposes in disguise of helping you out, so it is best to ignore the disclaimer at the bottom of the newsletters, as companies are paying them for exposure. But this does mean that many newsletters make a lot of false promises about companies who are far from the quality of the newsletter itself even.

3. Sell quickly. Take any profit you get and move on. Lingering in penny stock trading hasn't done anyone much good except gain loss. Once you have made over 20% to 30% profit, it is a good time to sell. Many traders, however, hope to gain far more, but getting too pumped up is a common mistake a lot of people make.

4. Don't listen to company management. This may sound weird, but in the murky world of penny stocks, don't always believe what you hear from companies. You should be picky about what you trust, especially companies that are biased towards their own stock. Many penny stocks are scams that work to enrich people from the inside, so it is best to do thorough research with sources that extend well beyond the business itself.

5. Don't sell short. Although short-pumping penny stocks may seem like a good idea, it is too volatile to consider. If you happen to be on the wrong side of the trade, you will be racking up quite a heavy loss. This strategy is best left when you have far more experience, but certainly not for people.

6. Focus only on penny stocks with high volume. They have higher chances of gaining a profit and success. Penny stocks that are traded more frequently and have a lot of activity is proof of higher liquidity.

7. Use mental stops. This is because the bid-ask spreads can potentially be high on penny stocks, and stop-losses can sometimes cause you to lose money from time to time. It is generally better to use mental stops.

8. Don't trade big. Basically, avoid the common pump and dump schemes that tend to circulate around penny stocks. A way to

identify this is by discovering the reason why penny stocks earnings are rising. Again, if you find no clear reason, it is likely to be a pump and dump scheme, where traders insert a large amount of money to inflate the sales, then sell all their stock, leaving the over-eager traders at a huge loss who jumped on board without double-checking their facts.

9. Don't fall in love with a stock. This means do not get emotionally attached to something you may have to let go of quickly. This may seem weird, but it is easy to get emotionally invested in something, especially if you spend a lot of time and research on a certain stock and possibly even the business itself. Companies market with an exciting story to keep you hooked, but this is exactly why you need to keep a personal distance from it all. Your strategy is to gain a profit, and sometimes it means letting go of stocks quickly and not taking part in whatever story they seem to be selling.

10. Finally, only buy the best of the bunch. Playing favoritism certainly works with penny stock investing, and it is best to purchase penny stocks that have had an earnings breakout. This is proof that companies are doing their job and are quite easy to find if you know where to look. Be aware of pump and dump schemes or scammers, as they can be mingled amongst the successful penny stocks.

10 Quick and Effective Tactics

Here are some of the proven and effective tactics you may want to consider when taking on penny stock investing. Keep in mind that you need to use these regarding what fits your circumstances best, or adapt them in such a way as is needed. These tactics are generic, and your scenarios are specific. Yet, it is handy to keep these tools at the ready and whip them out whenever you see an ideal scenario.

You can start off by calling the company. This does not mean to buy altogether what they are selling, but it is best to call a company you are indeed interested in investing in them. It is still ideal to also ask the necessary questions you may have, and verify if ever you can, and be in contact with some of the management or investor relations contact. You can still discover a lot about a company in a ten-to-twenty-minute phone call even after certain hours of research. But, again, be cautious, as it is best to filter what you can and see if you can verify what they tell you.

Average up, instead of averaging down. This is a common trick used by savvy investors, meaning they do tend to purchase more shares when their investments do happen to increase in price. When the first purchase is made, the rising prices instigate one's belief that there is greater potential for the company. Their position will increase when the stock rises because they averaged up, considering they did purchase more at a higher price. But who would mind paying for stocks that are moving in the right direction?

Many beginners in trading have the tendency of averaging down, which means they purchase shares when it starts to fall in value. Although the logic tends to focus on being able to buy a higher quantity, they lose sight of the fact that a share is not doing so well when the price starts to sink. So why would you want to buy more stock as its value is starting to fall? In this case, you are buying for a loss, especially considering you do not have a guarantee for it to turn around and head back up in value.

It is best not to mix up the market risk with company risk. There are two different risks involved when you are investing in any form of stock. They are company risk and market risk. Company risks normally involve anything that tends to be related to the stock of the corporation you happen to be investing in. Market risk is the downside of any shares and overall stock market declines. Basically, indirectly connected to the company you are invested in, but more a general risk that any trader is taking on. If there is an overall crash in the value of investments, then even the best-growing companies' share value will drop. There is practically nothing a company can do with this risk, as again, it is indirectly connected to them and depends on the direction of most companies and not simply theirs. This is something you must be aware of when investing in any company. There is the company risk and the overall risk of the market in its entirety. Now, this does not mean there is a ticking time bomb in the markets, but as shown before, it can happen.

Remember to try out the product and use the service of the company you are interested in investing in. Testing out a company's service or product is probably the most effective marketing research you can perform and can prove even more effective than analyzing the financial results of the business. This is especially important with penny stocks, as understanding how customers feel about a business can give a clear picture of how it could flourish or fail in the future. This way, you are also far more aware of the quality of the service they are selling or how well the product works. This can truly make or break a company, and so it is wise to be one step ahead in understanding whether they appeal to the market.

Study the competition. How a business can compete will also make or break a company. Businesses that have been successful for decades suddenly plummet because of their inability to stay up-to-date. The economy is extremely competitive, and with the rise of international businesses, many are not just competing on a local scale but also a global one. If businesses from international countries still work for cheaper or produce better products, time and again, the local products are bound to fail or decrease in size and value. Therefore, it is best to do your own research on how the competition is faring against the business you want to invest in. Looking up their competitive edge or how well they can keep themselves up-to-date is important in predicting their potential for success. This may seem like extra work, but it is necessary for penny stocks, where information is few and far between.

Again, paper trading. It is a tactic mentioned a few times, and one does not need to dive in too deeply, as the advantages have already been mentioned. You are just doing yourself a massive favor by diving in and using this tactic.

Even as a beginner, it is a great tactic to understand the life cycle of a corporate company. Being able to identify where the business is will help you to know whether you should even consider investing at this point and time.

All companies go through these cycles. It is inevitable. Many of them can extend a certain period within the business. However, history has proven this cycle time and again. Depending on the phase the company is in does depend on how you should treat its shares.

1. Start-up phase

2. Growth phase

3. Maturity phase

4. Decline phase

The positive side to this spectrum is that when a company does decline, it can always reinvent itself. By taking a step back, reevaluating, and adapting to begin the start-up phase again is normally what a good company does. A company needs to keep up with the competition, normally bringing something new and unique to the table.

Awareness of the corporate cycle will certainly go a long way for you to make the right investment decisions.

Finally, remember to take your time to understand what exactly is driving the share price. This may take some time to learn, but it should become easier. Remember to also monitor the short interest (the percentage of shares in a company that is held by short-sellers—the total number of shares that had finally been sold short by the investors, however, it had not yet been fully closed out or even covered). This is normally revealed in the form of a percentage. When it is shown in a percentage, it normally takes the shorted shares to the number of outstanding shares.

Shorting Stocks: What Does This Mean?

This normally refers to short selling, where the investment or trading strategy speculates that there is a decline in both stock and security prices. This is quite a complex strategy, best taken on by people who have had more experience when it comes to trading.

At the end of the day, all these trading tools and tactics are to help your journey along with penny stock trading, but it can never be an absolute guarantee. However, using these tactics can reduce a lot of mistakes and losses, and take your time incorporating them all. Also, respect yourself to the fact that you are completely new to all this, and it will take time to add everything you need to. So again, take your time, and remember to revisit the guides and books to brush up on anything that you may have forgotten.

Keep in mind that you are also a beginner, so when you choose your strategies and endgame, you must keep this in mind. Play the game of trades with a knowledge of your limitations, pushing yourself to become better and take on more tactics available in the trader's world. The more experience you build, the more profitable you are likely to become. Do not be afraid to push yourself, and just be aware when you cannot go any further, for now, anyway.

Conclusion

Now you know enough to kick-start your journey! Although there is truly so much more to learn, you now have the tools and equipment to discover it for yourself.

Penny stock investing is no easy feat, but it is not so insanely complex either. You may have noticed several key points that kept rising in the book, and they are indeed some solid factors that make or break your ultimate success.

As much as one can wish to guarantee that you will earn major profits, such promises are dangerous to make in the world of trade. But following this guide can certainly boost your potential, and that is a promise. Do not be afraid to revise or visit the guide again in order to brush up on forgotten facts and realities when it comes to penny stocks. Especially as you start out, repeating what you know and keeping the tactics sharp and fresh in your mind can help you make far healthier decisions. Additionally, keep the following in mind:

Do your research. Those three words are the main factors that help to make or break your trading career. Some follow others and simply earn by blind luck, only to suffer a loss or several losses if they continue to follow this pattern. Any savvy investor can tell you the key to standing out is by working for it. Even if it means doing five minutes of extra reading that most people would merely dismiss. This is where "doing your homework" pays off, and normally in a profitable way.

Remember the volatility and randomness in the market. It is best to be forgiving when you happen to fail an analysis, nor do things happen according to plan. As much as one could say that the market is fully predictable, that would be an outright lie. Accepting the randomness of the market, and preparing yourself emotionally, is building the stepping stones for a greater and longer trader's journey, where failure does not occur. Rather, these are mistakes that can be learned from.

Finally, never invest money you cannot afford to lose. This has been repeated more than once, but this is a factor you absolutely cannot ignore. Too many people have suffered by making this mistake; do not add your name to this list.

Keep in mind that penny stock investing requires a different approach to normal investing and traditionally is more hands-on. This means you will have to take more time and effort to earn profits in this category. In addition, this is a more volatile market, which means there is normally a greater amount of risk entailed to it. But the greater the risk, the greater the reward. However, be realistic about the level of profits that may stream in; otherwise, it may just lead to disappointment and giving up (which we certainly do not want).

Lastly, enjoy it! It is no use working an extensive and stressful journey in investing without finding some joy and happiness in the journey itself. So remember to keep smiling and cling to any form of positivity. Join a community of like-minded people, and do not be afraid to ask for their advice. However, remember they have their own biased views, and it would truly be best to filter between them for the rare gems that do come from people who have had experience.

Penny stock investing has small share prices with huge potential, and this is what you want to tap into. Practice having a trader's mentality when approaching this, and remember that you are not completely alone in this journey. Do not be afraid to adopt the strategies of others if you conclude they can work, and don't be afraid to stick to the plan or adapt it if circumstances do change.

At the end of the day, you are responsible for the income streaming your way. It is up to you and not the opinions of others to steer your investments forward. So, keep your chin up and stay up-to-date on the competition. It is best in the world of trading to stay ahead in the game, and that is something you should always be striving and working hard towards. Strive for growing and learning, not perfection, and you will already be far more ahead and aware than most traders. Penny stocks await you. So, are you ready to jump in today?

References

5 Best Penny Stocks To Buy Now & How to Develop a Strategy. (2017, September 20). Timothy Sykes. https://www.timothysykes.com/blog/best-penny-stocks/#How_to_Find_the_Best_Penny_Stocks_in_10_Steps

10 Rapid Result Tactics for Penny Stock Traders. (n.d.). Dummies. Retrieved July 31, 2021, from https://www.dummies.com/personal-finance/investing/penny-stocks/10-rapid-result-tactics-penny-stock-traders/

64 Penny Stock Trading Rules to Honor My $127,000 Profit Week. (2014, March 2). Timothy Sykes. https://www.timothysykes.com/blog/164-penny-stock-trading-rulestips-celebrate-164000-profit-week/

Advantages & Disadvantages of Penny Stock. (n.d.). Pocketsense. Retrieved July 31, 2021, from https://pocketsense.com/advantages-disadvantages-penny-stock-3471.html

Balance, F. B. F. L. P. L. wrote about penny stocks for T., Books, I. the A. of T., & Leeds, including "Penny S. for D. "R. T. B. editorial policies P. (n.d.). *Here Is a Step-By-Step Guide How to Get Started Trading Penny Stocks.* The Balance. https://www.thebalance.com/penny-stocks-trading-guide-for-beginners-4123635

Beginners Penny Stock Trading Strategy (momo). (2016, November 14). Warrior Trading. https://www.warriortrading.com/penny-stock-trading/

Buying Penny Stocks [Understanding Penny Stocks]. (n.d.). Www.pennystocks.org. Retrieved July 31, 2021, from http://www.pennystocks.org/buying-penny-stocks.php

Curtis, G. (2020, April 4). *Trading psychology: Why the mind matters in making money*. Investopedia. https://www.investopedia.com/articles/trading/02/110502.asp

Day Trading Tools | Penny Stock Tools & Resources | ClayTrader. (n.d.). Retrieved July 31, 2021, from https://claytrader.com/resources/

Emotional Trading: These 7 Emotions Can Destroy Your Dream! - DTTW. (2021, May 28). Day Trade the WorldTM. https://www.daytradetheworld.com/trading-blog/these-7-emotions-can-destroy-your-day-trading-dream/

finance, F. B. F. T. P. N. writes about all aspects of personal, Retirement, I. S. for, Wisely, I., & Nolan, being a smart consumer R. T. B. editorial policies P. (n.d.). *What Is a Penny Stock?* The Balance. Retrieved July 30, 2021, from https://www.thebalance.com/what-is-a-penny-stock-5114192

Getting a Good StockBroker [Understanding Penny Stocks]. (n.d.). Www.pennystocks.org. Retrieved July 31, 2021, from http://www.pennystocks.org/getting-a-good-stock-broker.php

Getting Started in Penny Stocks [Understanding Penny Stocks]. (n.d.). Www.pennystocks.org. Retrieved July 31, 2021, from http://www.pennystocks.org/getting-started-in-penny-stocks.php

Glossary of Terms Used [Understanding Penny Stocks]. (n.d.). Www.pennystocks.org. http://www.pennystocks.org/glossary-of-terms-used.php

Guides, T. S. (2019). Penny Stocks for Beginners. Trading With Just $100. *Tradingstrategyguides.com.* https://tradingstrategyguides.com/penny-stocks/

Hayes, A. (n.d.). *Candlestick.* Investopedia. https://www.investopedia.com/terms/c/candlestick.asp

Hayes, A. (2019). *A Breakdown on How the Stock Market Works.* Investopedia. https://www.investopedia.com/articles/investing/082614/how-stock-market-works.asp

How (and Where) To Find Penny Stocks To Buy. (n.d.). Wall Street Survivor. Retrieved July 31, 2021, from https://www.wallstreetsurvivor.com/starter-guides/find-penny-stock/

How To Day Trade Penny Stocks & 9 Important Strategies To Learn Now. (2021, January 31). Penny Stocks to Buy, Picks, News and Information | PennyStocks.com. https://pennystocks.com/featured/2021/01/31/how-to-trade-penny-stocks-9-important-strategies-to-learn-now/

How to Find Penny Stocks Pre-Spike (Step-by-Step Guide). (2019, June 26). Timothy Sykes. https://www.timothysykes.com/blog/my-secret-formula-for-finding-penny-stocks-pre-spike/#How_to_Pick_a_Potential_Penny_Stock_Winner_Pre-Spike-2

How To Invest In Penny Stocks - The Complete Step By Step Guide. (n.d.). Money under 30. Retrieved July 31, 2021, from https://www.moneyunder30.com/how-to-invest-in-penny-stocks

Investor Bulletin: Microcap Stock Basics (Part 1 of 3: General Information) | Investor.gov. (n.d.). Www.investor.gov. Retrieved July 30, 2021, from https://www.investor.gov/introduction-investing/general-resources/news-alerts/alerts-bulletins/investor-bulletins/investor-3

Investor Bulletin: Microcap Stock Basics (Part 2 of 3: Research) | Investor.gov. (n.d.). Www.investor.gov. Retrieved July 31, 2021, from https://www.investor.gov/introduction-investing/general-resources/news-alerts/alerts-bulletins/investor-bulletins-32

Keythman, B. (n.d.). *How to Compare Market Capitalization & Stockholders' Equity.* Finance - Zacks. Retrieved July 31, 2021, from https://finance.zacks.com/compare-market-capitalization-stockholders-equity-1812.html

Murphy, C. B. (2021, January 28). *How Penny Stocks Trade and How Investors Can Buy Them.* Investopedia. https://www.investopedia.com/terms/p/pennystock.asp

Penny Stock Chart Patterns Every Trader Should Know [Top 5]. (2019, June 19). Penny Stocks to Buy, Picks, News and Information | PennyStocks.com. https://pennystocks.com/featured/2019/06/19/penny-stock-chart-patterns-every-trader-should-know-top-5/

Penny Stocks for Day Trading: Beginner's Guide. (2020, December 23). StocksToTrade. https://stockstotrade.com/penny-stocks-for-day-trading/#Things_I_Look_for_in_Penny_Stocks_for_Day_Trading

Penny Stocks Trading Guide for Beginners [2020]. (2016, December 22). Warrior Trading. https://www.warriortrading.com/penny-stocks/

Should You Invest or Trade Penny Stocks? - Pros & Cons Of Penny Stocks. (2020, October 27). Rockwell Trading. https://www.rockwelltrading.com/coffee-with-markus/should-you-invest-in-penny-stocks/

Sincere, M. (n.d.). *10 ways to trade penny stocks.* MarketWatch. Retrieved July 31, 2021, from https://www.marketwatch.com/story/10-ways-to-trade-penny-stocks-2012-02-03

Step by Step Penny Stock Guide. (n.d.). Www.peterleeds.com. Retrieved July 31, 2021, from https://www.peterleeds.com/step-by-step-penny-stock-guide.htm

Stockopedia - Stock Screening, Ratings, & Portfolio Analysis. (n.d.). Stockopedia. Retrieved July 31, 2021, from http://www.stockopedia.com

stocks, F. B. F. L. P. L. is an expert on investing in, Planning, H. O. a D. of E. W. with F., derivatives, equities, Income, F., Management, P., Dummies, analytics H. is the author of several publications including "Penny S. for, Stocks, publishes the financial newsletter P. L. P., NBC, CBS, Fox, CNN, Today, R., & Leeds, several dozen other outlets P. attended the U. of W. R. T. B. editorial policies P. (n.d.). *Pros and Cons of Penny Stock Investing.* The Balance. https://www.thebalance.com/the-pros-and-cons-of-penny-stocks-2637072

The First Deadly Sin Of The Penny Stock Trader: Greed. (n.d.). Www.meta-Formula.com. Retrieved July 31, 2021, from https://www.meta-formula.com/penny-stock-trader.html

The Pros and Cons of Trading Penny Stocks. (2019, May 31). Modest Money. https://www.modestmoney.com/pros-cons-trading-penny-stocks/

Trading Psychology: How to Get Into a Successful Mindset. (2018, February 28). Timothy Sykes. https://www.timothysykes.com/blog/improve-trading-psychology

trading, F. B. F. L. F. T. C. M. is a financial writer with over 13 years experience creating markets-related content H. is an expert in, Analysis, T., & Murphy, C. received a bachelor's degree in finance from the U. of A. L. about our editorial policies C. (n.d.). *How to Invest in Penny Stocks for Beginners*. Investopedia. Retrieved July 31, 2021, from https://www.investopedia.com/articles/investing/091114/how-invest-penny-stocks.asp

Where Do Penny Stocks Trade? [Understanding Penny Stocks]. (n.d.). Www.pennystocks.org. Retrieved July 31, 2021, from http://www.pennystocks.org/where-do-penny-stocks-trade.php

Why Trade Penny Stocks? 4 Simple Reasons Why. (2018, December 13). StocksToTrade. https://stockstotrade.com/why-trade-penny-stocks/

Yahoo Finance - Business Finance, Stock Market, Quotes, News. (2015). @YahooFinance. http://finance.yahoo.com

Image Referencing:

AbsolutVision. (n.d.). *No Risk No Reward.*
https://Pixabay.com/Illustrations/Dices-Over-Newspaper-
Profit-2656028/.

Chen, J. (2019). *Penny Stocks Short Selling.* Investopedia.
https://www.investopedia.com/terms/s/shortselling.asp

Hassan, M. (n.d.-a). *Candle Charts.*
https://Pixabay.com/Vectors/Business-Forex-Stock-Chart-
Trading-5477997/.

Hassan, M. (n.d.-b). *Stay Focused.*
https://Pixabay.com/Illustrations/Visa-Virtual-Visa-Credit-
Card-3349340/.

Hassan, M. (n.d.-c). *You Need A Plan.*
https://Pixabay.com/Vectors/Training-Course-Business-
Session-5822607/.

Mediamodifier. (n.d.). *Downside of Penny Stocks -Graph
Growth Process.* https://Pixabay.com/Illustrations/Graph-
Growth-Progress-Diagram-3078546/.

Openartclipvectors. (n.d.). *Do's and Dont's.*
https://Pixabay.com/Vectors/Business-Commerce-
Decisions-1297332/.

OpenClipart Vectors. (n.d.). *Trader Toolbox.*
https://Pixabay.com/Vectors/Briefcase-Toolbox-Box-Tools-
157280/.

OpenClipartvectors. (n.d.). *Research is Key*.
https://Pixabay.com/Vectors/Papers-Stack-Heap-
Documents-576385/.

Tumisu. (n.d.). *Mental Battle of a Trader*.
https://Pixabay.com/Illustrations/Mental-Health-Psychology-
Psychiatry-2313428/.